How to
TRIM, GROOM and SHOW
YOUR DOG

by

BLANCHE SAUNDERS
and other authorities

(New edition of the book
formerly titled
*"Grooming and Showing
Instructions"*)

Illustrated

1963
HOWELL BOOK HOUSE INC.
575 Lexington Avenue
New York 22, N. Y.

Foreword

Despite the large number of dog books being published today, there is still need for a few down-to-earth, authoritative books designed to help the newcomer. This is one such book. Its presentation is straightforward and practical and the helpful illustrations, in addition to being excellent visual aids, are interesting and informative. Much will be learned about the many breeds so completely covered from the description of how the ideal dog of each breed should look. With the help of this book the novice need no longer learn how to prepare a dog for exhibition the embarrassing hard way.

The non-exhibitor can find good use for this book too. A well groomed dog is a pride and joy and a pleasure to live with. He need not be in a show ring to feel fit and look like the fine representative of his breed he really is.

The right way is not only the best but usually the easiest— certainly the most rewarding. The staff of authorities that made this book possible are an assurance that the methods and practices outlined are proper and accepted procedure. They can be followed by readers with assurance and satisfaction in the well being and appearance of their dogs.

JOE STETSON

Dog Editor of *Field and Stream*

TABLE OF CONTENTS

'In good name and fame with the very best.'

2 *Henry IV*. II. 4. 82

Showing Your Dog

HAVE YOU EVER watched a dog show
and thought it would be fun to exhibit your own dog? Dog
showing is the hobby of thousands of people who show their
one and only pet for the thrill and excitement of competition. You, too, can have this experience and there is the
possibility you will win a blue ribbon for your dog and ful-
fill your dream of making him a champion or gaining his
obedience degrees.

You must not confuse a local or neighborhood pet show
with a *licensed dog show* or *obedience trial.* Pet shows are
informal affairs and may be sponsored by anyone. Licensed
shows are held under the jurisdiction of The American
Kennel Club and the rules are rigidly enforced. There are
eight to nine hundred licensed shows held annually and from
ten to 2500 dogs compete at each show. As these figures would
indicate, the dog business is not to be taken lightly. It is the
fourth largest industry in the United States.

Dog showing can run into a lot of money or it can be an
inexpensive pastime. If you employ a professional handler
to show your dog, you can expect to pay him twenty to
thirty dollars a show for his services. If the handler travels
extensively, as most of them do, the cost may be even more.

The professional handler is a luxury but he knows his business and can be depended upon to set the dog down in the best possible form and to present the dog's merits effectively. The majority of dog owners, however, prefer to attend local dog shows and to handle their dogs themselves. While they are handicapped when it comes to competing against the professional, they enjoy the pleasant and exciting experience of taking part in the show and if they win, it is all the more glamorous.

The novice exhibitor with an inexperienced dog will do some wishful thinking. However, it would be surprising if he won top awards in his first all-breed bench show. In obedience, this can and very often does happen. The dogs are judged on performance and very often a novice dog, in the few simple exercises, will receive a higher score than will the fully trained dog in the more complicated tests. The vast majority of dog show exhibitors, however, take home a ribbon, a trophy, or some other special prize. Prizes are not valuable in the monetary sense, for cash awards are small. If an exhibitor wins back his entry fee, he considers himself lucky. In obedience, completing a dog's degree or gaining a leg thereon is sufficient reward for a day of hard work. There is a fascination about exhibiting one's own dog and receiving an award, however small, that keeps dog shows popular and exhibitors enthusiastic.

First, let us talk about the breed ring. It is assumed that your dog is purebred and reasonably typical of his breed, but before you even think about going to a dog show, you should be aware of any disqualifying features your dog may have that would eliminate him immediately from competition.

It would be impractical to list here the disqualifications for every breed of dog, so we suggest you write to The American Kennel Club, 221 Park Avenue South, New York 3, N.Y., and ask for the address of the secretary of the breed club in which you are interested, or ask The American Kennel Club to send you a copy of the breed Standard. With this list of the desirable and undesirable points, you will know before you enter your first dog show whether your dog is a good specimen or if, because of his many poor features, you cannot be hopeful of winning with him.

When you write The American Kennel Club about your breed, ask for a copy of the rules and regulations governing dog shows. If you are interested in obedience trials, request the booklet that will tell you all about them. Dog show rules are strict for both the owner and the dog. If either you or your dog fail to meet the requirements, you might as well know it before entering a show.

Perhaps you are wondering why so many good looking and well-trained dogs never attend a dog show. The answer is simple. Some owners do not know how good their dogs really are. Others do not care—the dog is a family pet and the owner is no more interested in showing than he is in entering into a contest himself. Still other owners are deterred from exhibiting by their lack of knowledge of dog shows and dog show procedure. Showing a dog in either breed or obedience is a simple matter. Most exhibitors are comparative newcomers to the sport, with as many as half having shown their dogs for the first time less than a year before. If you own a dog and want to take him to a show, it will not take you long to learn the tricks of the trade and before you know it, you will feel and act like a professional.

Before you do enter your dog in a show, read this book carefully. Attend as many shows as you can as a spectator. Watch the other exhibitors and listen to their comments. Before making the plunge into a licensed trial, take your dog to a sanctioned match for experience, especially for practice in obedience. Sanctioned matches are run according to the rules of The American Kennel Club except that wins do not count toward the dog's championship or toward his obedience degrees. Almost every local kennel club holds sanctioned trials as well as informal practice matches several times a year, thus providing a golden opportunity for the exhibitor and his dog. There is no better way to learn about dogs than to handle them; no better way to discover the ins and outs of a dog show than to become a part of one.

Championship and Obedience Degrees

THE DOGS of our country are divided into Groups, according to breed. The American Kennel Club recognizes six major Groups and well over one hundred different breeds. If you have an Irish Setter, for instance, he belongs in the Sporting Group, along with the other bird dogs. If he is a German Shepherd Dog, he automatically falls into the Working Group, because these dogs have been bred to perform special services. The Dachshund and Beagle, both members of the Hound family, belong in the Hound Group, where the dogs are specialists when it comes to hunting rabbits and other fur-bearing animals. Terriers, whether Irish, Wire-haired, or Kerry Blue, are in the Terrier Group, whose members like nothing better than to ferret out underground rodents. There is also a Toy Group for small dogs like the Chihuahua. And last, but not least, the Non-Sporting Group for breeds like the Bulldog, Chow Chow, Dalmatian, and Poodle.

So that you will further understand dog shows and how dogs become champions, let us explain the classifications for the individual breeds. There are five basic classes: *Puppy* (for dogs under a year old); *Novice* (for dogs that have never won a blue ribon except in the *Puppy Class*); *American-Bred* (for dogs whelped in the United States);

Bred-By-Exhibitor (for dogs owned and being shown by the person who bred them); and a classification called *Open* (open to all). When you glance over the premium list, which is the advance notice of a dog show, these are the classes you will see listed. At a *Specialty Show* (this is for only one breed of dog) you will have even a wider selection. Each of these classes is further subdivided by sex so that males and females are shown separately. In dog show language, males are called dogs and females, bitches. An exhibitor is immediately earmarked as an amateur if he hesitates to use the word bitch when referring to a female dog. Another mistake novice dog owners make is calling a dog a "thoroughbred." That term applies to horses only. When you speak of a registered dog, call him a purebred.

But to get back to how a dog becomes a champion! The winners of the Puppy, Novice, American-Bred, Bred-By-Exhibitor, and Open Classes compete in a *Special* Class against each other. If the dogs are competing, it is called the *Winners' Dog Class.* If bitches, it is the *Winners' Bitch Class.* In each case, the winners of the Winners' Dog Class and the Winners' Bitch Class are the *only* dogs of their breed that day to receive championship points. The number of points awarded depends upon the breed involved and varies from show to show. The most points a dog can win in any one show is five. The least number is one. To become a champion, an accumulated total of fifteen points must be won under at least three different judges, and two of the wins must be "majors" (three points or more). At every show then, we have a Winners' Dog, who, if he has competition, wins championship points, a Winners' Bitch, who does the same. These two then compete against each other for *Best of Winners,* and whoever takes first place has the opportunity to enter the *Specials Only Class* and compete against the dogs and bitches that are already champions.

There are technicalities that will arise from time to time and about which you will learn as you go along. For instance, if the Winners' Dog receives two points and the Winners' Bitch five at a particular show, when they come up against one another, if the dog places over the bitch, the bitch keeps the five points she won but the dog, instead of the two points awarded to him for going Winners' Dog, receives the same number of points as the bitch—in this case, five.

Another common occurrence, and one which you might not understand, is how a second place winner can be awarded the *Reserve Winners'* ribbon over dogs that have taken a blue. Blue indicates the dog took first prize. Let us assume that when the winning Puppy, Novice, American-Bred, Bred-By-Exhibitor, and Open dogs competed against each other in the Winners' class, the American-Bred took first. There is a second award in this class called *Reserve Winners' Dog.* If the judge decides he likes the dog who placed second in the American-Bred class better than the winning dogs of the other classes, he will award the ribbon to this dog, providing he has not been beaten by the other dogs. The Reserve Winners' Dog award is made in case the Winner's Dog should later be disqualified for any one of many reasons. The Reserve Winners' Dog then automatically receives the winning points.

You will notice dogs listed in the dog show catalog under *Exhibition Only.* This means that the dog will not compete that day but by paying an entry fee the owner is permitted to have his dog on exhibition, a practice common among kennel owners when they have a dog at stud and want other people to see him. Dogs in transit are frequently entered in this class, for this allows them to be on the show grounds without going through the procedure of being judged.

Before we go on, let us take time to review the important facts. In the average dog show there are five classifications for dogs and five for bitches. There are four placings in each of the classes. A blue ribbon is first; red is second; yellow is third; and white is fourth. The first place winners of each class compete against one another, and a purple ribbon is given to the winner. This means the dog (or bitch) is the best male (or female) of all those competing in the classes that day. He (or she) receives points toward his (or her) championship; the number of points depends upon the number of dogs (or bitches) of the breed present and the part

12

of the country in which the show is held. The second place winner receives a purple and white ribbon marked *Reserve Winners' Dog* (or *Bitch*), which means the dog is the second best male (or female) of all those competing in the classes that day. The best male then competes against the best bitch and the winner receives a blue and white ribbon for *Best of Winners'*. The holder of this award is the one who competes in the *Specials Only Class* against the champions.

Any number of champions may be entered in the *Specials Only Class*, but only one will be named *Best of Breed*. This may be either a dog or a bitch and the ribbon is purple and gold. If there are varieties of the breed, as in Poodles, the winner is called *Best of Variety*. If the Best of Breed (or Best of Variety) winner is a dog, a bitch will be picked as *Best of Opposite Sex* and she does not necessarily have to be a champion. The ribbon is red and white. If a bitch should win Best of Breed (or Best of Variety) a male is selected to receive the red and white rosette.

Earlier we mentioned the six Groups into which all breeds are divided. All Best of Breed or Best of Variety winners have the opportunity to compete against the other breeds of dogs in their respective Group. Here, again, there are four placings and the ribbons, although more elaborate, are the same colors as in the classes: blue, red, yellow, and white. The winning dogs of the six Groups then compete against each other for *Best Dog in Show*. Until 1962, if a dog born outside the United States won Best in Show, some shows offered an award for *Best American-Bred in Show*. If whelped in the United States, the dog that placed second in a group to the *Best Dog in Show* was eligible to compete for *Best American-bred in Show*. Since American-breds were more than holding their own with the imports, the "consolation prize" was stopped.

Certain breeds of dogs, though recognized by The American Kennel Club, have not as yet gained popularity and hence the breeds are not well represented at dog shows. Many times there will be only one exhibit of a breed and in this case, the dog automatically receives *Best of Breed* and

13

becomes eligible for competition in the Group. The dog does not receive championship points because he had no competition, but if he should place first in the Group, he will receive the maximum number of points awarded to any breed in his Group that day.

Winning obedience degrees is a little different from making your dog a bench show champion. The three obedience titles offered by The American Kennel Club are C. D. (Companion Dog); C. D. X. (Companion Dog Excellent); and U. D. (Utility Dog). There is still a fourth called T. D., which means Tracking Dog, but the tracking test is held apart from dog shows. While the first three degrees are progressive, the tracking title may be won at any time.

In order to qualify for a leg on an obedience title, the dog must pass a series of tests in which he receives a score of 170 points or more out of a possible 200. He must receive more than 50% for each of the required exercises and he must win three legs under three different judges. A certain number of dogs must be in competition or the win does not count. The number of dogs varies in different parts of the country.

Just as in breed shows, there are five basic classes in obedience: Novice A (for amateurs); Novice B (for amateurs or professionals); Open A (for amateurs); Open B (for amateurs or professionals); and Utility (for amateurs and professionals). In a Specialty Show that features only obedience, there may be additional classes such as *Graduate Novice, Brace, Team* and *Versatility*. These last four increase the number of entries and make the show more interesting from the spectators' point of view, but they have no bearing on the dogs' obedience degrees.

There is one big difference between making a dog a bench show champion and winning his obedience titles. The obedience trained dog can enter the required number of shows under the rules of The American Kennel Club and win his obedience degrees without actually placing in the ribbons. The dog does not have to win over the other dogs in his class as he does in breed, but merely receive the qualifying scorces. However, more about obedience in a later chapter.

14

The Show Itself

IF YOU ARE wondering about dog shows and how they are run, the explanation is simple. There are superintendents licensed by The American Kennel Club who make a business of putting on dog shows. The superintendent works with the sponsor of the show to stage an affair that will appeal to both the exhibitor and the spectator. At the same time, the rules of The American Kennel Club must be enforced.

When a local dog club wishes to put on a show, its first act is to request permission from The American Kennel Club, which must approve the date, the location, the judges (judges are sometimes invited six months or more in advance), and all details as to classes and prizes offered. Permission granted, the sponsoring dog club seeks the assistance of a superintendent, who may agree to run the show for a set fee or on a percentage basis.

The superintendent prints the premium list and mails it to the dog owners in the show area in advance of the show. He furnishes the ribbons and prints the catalog that lists the dogs in their respective classes. If the local kennel club wishes to economize, it does some of the work itself, turning certain details over to the superintendent. This is often the case with a specialty club show (a single breed or an all-obedience show) or when the show is unbenched and the dogs are not required to be on display. The premium list will state whether the show is benched or not. If it is, the rule is very strict about dogs' remaining in their stalls during the hours of the show. If a dog is not being exhibited, being prepared for exhibition, or being exercised, he *must* be on his bench. Failure to comply may result in a fine or a possible suspension by The American Kennel Club.

There are other dog show rules with which you should be familiar. A dog that is blind, deaf, or lame is automatically barred from competition. Cryptorchids, monorchids, castrated males, and spayed bitches may be shown in obedience but not in breed. On the other hand, bitches in season may be shown in breed but not in obedience. In the breed ring, a dog's color or markings may not be changed by the use of any substance. Chalk may be used on a white dog for the purpose of cleaning his coat but it must be brushed out thoroughly before the dog is exhibited.

Every dog entered in a show must be registered or in the process of being registered with The American Kennel Club. By paying a twenty-five cent fee at the time he makes his entry, an owner may *list* an unregistered dog provided it is eligible for registration. But, with so many dogs arriving in the United States from foreign countries, it is just as well to know that a *listed* dog may be shown only three times. After that, the dog must be registered or special permission must be granted if the dog is to continue his show ring career. Even though a dog receives the required number of championship points and the necessary legs for his obedience degrees, he must be registered with the A. K. C. or the certificates acknowledging his wins will be withheld. When you buy a dog, pay special attention to the dog's eligibility for registration in this country.

If you are wondering where and when dog shows are held, write to The American Kennel Club and ask for the name and address of the superintendent who handles the shows in your part of the country. Then write to the superintendent and request that your name be placed on the mailing list so you will receive advance notice of the shows.

16

Dog publications usually list forthcoming shows and you can write to the breed club secretary for further information.

When you receive your premium list, read it carefully. It will tell you the date of the show, the place it will be held, and whether the show is benched or unbenched. It will state the entry fee and give the closing date for entries, after which no changes may be made or entries cancelled. The premium list gives the names of the judges and their assignments and names the prizes and special awards that are being offered.

If you decide to enter your dog in a particular show, fill out the entry blank at the back of the premium list and mail it (ith the required fee) so it will reach the superintendent's office before the closing date. Exhibitors are usually allowed ten days in which to register, but in a large show entries are sometimes limited, so do not wait until the last minute or your entry may be returned and the show you planned to attend will go on without you.

As time goes on and you are really bitten by the dog show bug, you will find yourself traveling more afield and attending more and more shows. This means traveling by plane and train as well as by car and staying in hotels or motels. Not every place will accept dogs and the rules about taking dogs on public conveyances are very strict. It is suggested that you make reservations where you know you will be welcome, and check with railway and airline officials as to their requirements. The premium list for a show usually gives names and addresses of places where exhibitors may stay with their dogs. Gaines Dog Research Center, 250 Park Avenue, New York City, has compiled a list of places throughout the fifty States where dogs are accepted. This pamphlet, called *Touring with Towser,* is available for a modest fee.

We all, at some time or another, get caught on the road without reservations. It is a good idea to carry a folding crate for such an emergency. If the place at which you hope to stay refuses to take dogs, perhaps you can make arrangements to stay anyway by offering to keep the dog in the crate. Especially, if you leave sufficient deposit to pay for any damages. One handler makes this a regular practice whether he travels for pleasure or to attend dog shows.

For long trips by car, a fifty-foot clothesline will be useful for exercising your dog, for it will preclude the possibility of losing him through accident or by his running away. When you park your car in hot weather, select a shady spot and *leave the windows partly open.* Many dogs die every year as the result of being confined in a closed car that has been parked in the glaring sun.

A few days prior to the show, you will receive an identification card that gives the entry number of your dog. This is also your dog's bench number and should be taken to the show so he can be admitted. The ticket of admission, which accompanies the identification card and the program of the judging, is for your own use and permits you to enter the show grounds without paying. If you have one or two dogs, you will receive one admission ticket. If several members of your family go to the dog show with you, they will have to pay admission.

Speaking of taking things to a show, when you become an exhibitor, pack a bag with the items you will need and keep it handy and ready to go at a moment's notice. Here are a few things you must have: show leash, bench chain, collar, tools (such as a brush, comb, scissors, etc.), and identification card and admission ticket. Here are some other things you will find useful: towels, newspapers, a sponge, food (on a long trip), feeding pan, can opener, cooked liver or a toy to attract the dog's attention when he is being shown, glycerine suppositories (if away overnight), Bismuth Subnitrate (for treating diarrhea), thermos, grooming table or crate, safety pins, elastic bands, and a first aid kit.

Obedience exhibitors would do well to gather together their scent articles, the seek-back articles, the dumbbell, chain collar, leash, etc., the night before the show and put them where they will not be forgotten in the rush of leaving for the show. It is easy to hurry off and fifteen miles

18

from home remember the dumbbell you left on the kitchen table.

For the pleasure and convenience of the exhibitor himself, here are more items that can be used to advantage: sweater (it may be chilly at the show, even in summer), blanket, raincoat, rubbers, a thermos for hot or cold drinks, lunch kit, folding chair and portable radio, and for outdoor shows in warm weather, a beach umbrella. As long as you spend your week-ends at dog shows, you might as well be comfortable!

If you are attending your first show, allow plenty of time to reach your destination. You must be present by a specfied hour or you will have made the trip for nothing. Most shows close their doors at 11:30 A. M. and late arrivals, no matter what they do, are unable to get in. Perhaps your breed will have been scheduled to be judged at 10:00 o'clock. If you are not there, the judge will not wait for you. It will be to your advantage to start a few minutes early so you can arrive at the show relaxed and with plenty of time to prepare your dog for the ring. En route to the show, watch for arrows which indicate the direction to take. Some shows are poorly marked or have no markings at all, but, for the most part, instructions are adequate. If you are like most of us, you will heave a sigh of relief when you spot the dog show sign that indicates you are going in the right direction.

With experience you will learn to keep your dog's identification card and your ticket of admission where you can reach them at a moment's notice. You will remember to have the dog examined by the veterinarian and the identification card stamped so the dog will be admitted to the ring. You will memorize your dog's entry number in case it is announced over the loud speaker system and so you will know which bench to look for when you enter the show grounds. You will locate the ring where your dog will be judged, should you have to rush at the last moment. And you will take mental note of the location of the superintendent's office, the water supply, the rest rooms, and the exercising pen for your dog.

If you carry a crate or a grooming table, it must be set up in the space allotted to handlers and their equipment. This may be in a separate tent at an outdoor show or in a special section of the building at an indoor show. Crates and tables are not permitted in the aisles and the grooming of one's dog must take place in the handlers' section or in the dog's stall.

Inside the show grounds, locate your benching stall and fasten your dog to it. Use a bench chain, for the dog might chew his leather leash and escape. The bench chain is designed with a snap on each end—one to snap to the dog's collar and one to secure him to the ring on the bench. Fasten the dog short so he cannot jump off. When you leave your dog for any length of time, ask a fellow exhibitor to watch him, then check back occasionally to see that everything is all right. Dog show people are extremely helpful when they see a dog entangled in his chain or hanging in his collar, and many a dog's life has been saved because of the quick thinking of a stranger. But accidents will happen when there is no one about and every precaution should be taken.

For the women, it is hoped you have left your valuables at home. In case you have not, do not leave your pocketbook unguarded. During the excitement of a dog show, you will forget your usual caution. Put your money, car keys, and other items of value in a small change purse and fasten it on your person. Tuck your pocketbook out of sight or ask someone to hold it while you are exhibiting, or preparing your dog for the ring.

It is assumed your dog was exercised before entering the show grounds, so if you give him a drink of water, and a blanket to sleep on, you may attend to other matters. Buy a catalog and see if your dog is entered correctly in his class or classes. While you are about it, write your name on the catalog. Look at the judging schedule and estimate how long it will be before your dog will be called into the ring. Since long-haired dogs require considerable grooming, you must watch the progress the judge is making and allow plenty of time to get your dog in shape.

Do not sit back and wait to have your dog called into the ring! On the other hand, do not keep the dog standing around for hours because you are over-anxious. Check in at the judging ring when the judge starts your breed. Tell the stewards (they are the people who assist the judge) that you are on the show grounds and where you can be found when you are not at your bench. Every attempt is made to locate an exhibitor if he fails to appear on time, but frequently these attempts are not successful. Often an exhibitor has been left grooming his dog within sight of the ring while the class went on without him.

A final word of caution: when you walk your dog through the aisles, hold him on a short leash and keep to the center of the lane. Dogs frequently lunge out and your dog could be bitten badly. As a matter of fact, be on guard every minute of the time to prevent your dog from being stepped on, bumped against, or attacked by other dogs, and from stepping on lighted cigarettes. Keep your dog calm and cool and apart from other dogs. Relax, yourself, and you will enter the judging ring with everything in your favor.

The Judging Ring

NOW FOR THE JUDGING! When you arrive at the entrance to the ring, an attendant will give you an arm band bearing the entry number of your dog. Place the band on your left arm and fasten it securely with the safety pin or elastic band you previously tucked away in your pocket. Men exhibitors are fortunate in that in their regular clothing they have several pockets for items such as a safety pin, a small comb, or a piece of cooked liver. Women handlers should buy a "dog show dress," which usually has pockets and is designed for the comfort of the wearer. There is a lot of stooping and bending to be done at a dog show, so use good judgment when making your selection!

When the class is assembled, the judge will ask the handlers to parade their charges counter-clockwise around the ring. This means the dog is on the handler's left side where the judge can see him. One place in line is as good as another unless you have a fast moving dog and get caught behind a plodder. In this case, go by him. When you pose your dog for individual examination, it does not help to jockey into any particular position in line. The winning dogs can be selected from any position. It does help, though, to keep

22

your dog apart from the others. If he is hemmed in, he may be overlooked during the judging.

In spite of little experience, the novice exhibitor can give the impression that he is a professional by following a few simple suggestions:

Watch your dog but keep one eye on the judge so you will not be caught napping.

Watch the other exhibitors! If they turn their dogs to face a certain way, turn yours in the same direction.

Do not stand so you block the judge's view. This is your dog's day. Remember?

Keep your dog moving or in a posed position while you are in the ring. If the class is a large one, let your dog relax, then re-pose him when the judge is examining the dog next to yours.

While you pose your dog, do not stand or crouch too close to him. Crowding puts the dog at a disadvantage.

Pose your dog quickly and fuss about minor details later. One quick method is to hold the dog's muzzle in your right hand; reach over the dog's back and place the left front foot with your left hand; switch hands; hold the muzzle in the left and place the right front foot with the right hand. Switch hands again! Reach under the body with the left hand and pose the left back leg; using the same hand, place the right back leg. If the tail should be carried up or out, get it in place immediately.

Place your dog's front foot by grasping his elbow. Do not take hold of his paw. Turn the head slightly to the right when you place the left front foot and slightly to the left when it is the right one you are moving. Pose the back legs by supporting the stifle joints.

Stroke your dog gently along his back or under his stomach while he is posing. This will keep him quiet for a longer period of time.

If the dog becomes restless, hook the little finger of your right hand under the collar on the dog's throat and rest his muzzle in your hand. The slight pressure of the collar on the back of his neck will prevent the dog from drawing back and getting out of hand.

When you gait your dog (this means moving him so the judge can see his style of trot) wad the leash into a ball and hold it in your left hand. Keep your elbows straight and the dog away from your body. Step out in a good stride without running (unless you are showing a breed such as the German Shepherd Dog that requires speed) or taking little mincing steps. Select the trot most suited to your dog and *keep his nose off the ground!*

It is hoped you will have trained your dog to gait on your right side as well as on your left! A switch-over will be necessary when the judge asks for a side-view action.

Avoid running down the dog ahead. This trick is used by some to make the opposition lose stride, but it is not a sporting thing to do. Neither does it enhance your own dog's appearance.

If you feel you are not showing your dog to advantage because he is hemmed in by some other dog, move to another spot. Unless the judge has indicated your position, he will not mind if you change.

Carry a piece of cooked liver in your pocket to use in attracting your dog's attention. If food does not work, use a small toy instead.

On a hot day at an outdoor show, protect your dog from the glaring sun. Use your own body to give him shade.

Except for a small brush or comb for long-coated dogs, leave the grooming implements on the grooming table. Constant fussing detracts from a dog's appearance.

No dog is perfect but we can show your dogs to the best advantage. There are ways to minimize a dog's faults and the amateur can learn them as well as the professional. In the grooming, it is hoped the charts and instructions in this book will make the owner's task a pleasure and give him satisfactory results. A few other tricks of the trade:

If a dog has excessive loose skin on his throat, place the leash close behind the dog's ears and hold it taut to keep the skin from sagging.

If the dog is "out at the elbows," show the dog on a tight leash to keep his weight off the front legs.

If the dog has flat feet when the Standard calls for well arched ones, lift up on the dog's stomach and push his weight forward.

Level the roached back (one that curves upward) by rubbing along the dog's spine to make him pull it down.

The hollow back can be straightened by lifting on the underside of the stomach and patting it lightly to make the dog hold it in place and hold his back straight.

If your dog draws back when you pose him, practice at home with the dog standing on a bench, his back feet close to the edge. Hold the dog's muzzle and try to push him over backward. Fear of dropping into space should make the dog draw forward and when you hold his muzzle in the show ring, he will respond in the same way.

We cannot all win, but when the ribbons are passed out, accept gracefully the one you receive. A smile and a courteous "thank you" may help the judge remember you another time. If your dog does not win, it is equally essential that you accept defeat gracefully.

If your dog wins one of the classes and has not been defeated in any of the others, stay around. He will compete later in the Winners' Class. If he takes first again, he will compete for Best of Winners', and if your dog is still lucky and wins there, he will compete against the champions for Best of Breed or Best of Variety. A Best of Breed winner, although eligible to compete in the Group, is not obliged to do so. If he should enter the Group and win, it is obligatory for the dog to enter the finals for Best in Show.

One rule generally accepted at dog shows is that an exhibitor must never question the judge. But, what better way for the novice to learn about his breed or about his dog's training than to ask the advice of those persons whose know-ledge is such that The American Kennel Club has seen fit to grant them a judging license? Providing the question is not argumentative nor of infinitesimal importance, an exhibitor, having paid his six to eight dollar entry fee, is entitled to ask a judge where his dog could be improved upon in body structure; or why, perhaps, the dog failed in obedience competition. Some kindly words of advice may make all the difference at the next show and, you may rest assured, there will be a next!

In the long history of dog shows it would be foolish to say that no dishonesty has ever occurred. For the most part, since a judge's reputation rests upon his integrity, he wants to do a good job. It cannot be said that there is no incom-petent judging. Decisions rest entirely on the opinion of the judge and different judges have different senses of value. A judge may be sold a bill of goods through ignorance, or he may be influenced by some other exhibitor. The judge's liking for a person may reflect in his liking for a dog. The differences in comparative merits of two dogs are frequently very small. One dog will win over another by a mere tech-nicality. In another show, the decision may be reversed, which goes to prove that when an exhibitor wins he should be delighted but not gloat. When he loses, he should feel sad but not despair.

Showing Your Dog in the Obedience Ring

YOU MAY have read about obedience trials or watched them at a dog show and wondered how one goes about preparing his dog for competition. The ideal way is to enroll your dog in a training class and learn how to do the training yourself. A professional trainer can teach your dog the exercises, but if you plan to handle the dog in the obedience ring, you will have more luck if you train him from the beginning. Training classes are usually sponsored by Humane Societies, dog clubs, schools, or some other body of civic-minded people. The course lasts from nine to twelve weeks, during which time the owner, under the guidance of an instructor, learns how to train his dog.

If there is a training club in your neighborhood, you might want to join that. Although you may not always agree with all the club's policies, you will profit through your association with the members. You will learn about dogs and dog shows. You may even have the experience of helping to put on a show yourself. You will discover short cuts in training to overcome problems and, through your doggie contacts, will form lifelong friendships.

The *Gazette,* the official publication of The American Kennel Club, lists affiliated training clubs throughout the United States. For information about those not connected with the A. K. C., ask local kennel owners, pet shop proprietors, or your own veterinarian.*

As stated previously, with few exceptions dog show rules that apply to the breed ring apply to the obedience classes. We have already mentioned that a bitch in season may be exhibited in breed. But this is to remind you that under no circumstances may she be shown in obedience. Spayed bitches, castrated males, and cryptorchids and monorchids, while automatically disqualified from the breed classes, are permitted to participate in obedience trials. Rulings as to the dog's color, size and weight for his breed, or, in the case of the Poodle, the style of clip, have no bearing when the dog is being shown in obedience. The dog is being judged on his ability to perform a series of exercises designed to test his response to the handler's commands, but he must still be a purebred dog.

Putting a dog through the C. D. or even the C. D. X. degree is relatively simple. Gaining the U. D. or the Tracking title can cause many a heartache. Though able to perform the more complicated exercises at home, a dog may not have had sufficient training to work under conditions that prevail at dog shows.

The booklet *Regulations and Standards for Obedience Trials,* published by The American Kennel Club, is the final word when it comes to obedience. Every obedience enthusiast, if he plans to enter his dog in obedience trials, should request a copy, for it outlines the procedure in the ring and gives full details on what the dog and handler must do to gain an obedience degree or a leg thereon.

Presuming, of course, that you have trained your dog to the best of your ability (and do not enter him unless he is ready) and have read and reread the latest A. K. C. rule book (the rules are revised occasionally, so make certain your copy is up to date), let us see what you can do to help your dog get his degrees as easily as possible.

---

* *The Complete Novice Obedience Course,* published by Howell Book House, the publisher of this book, is an excellent text for the novice who does not have access to organized obedience courses.

First of all, attend as many sanctioned matches as you can. The entry fee is usually one dollar, which is low compared to the six to eight dollar fee at a regular trial. For this amount, you will have a chance to see what your dog can do and perhaps make a correction so the dog will not become ringwise.

Lacking the opportunity to attend a sanctioned match, or even an inter-club match, the home or classroom training area should be set up to resemble a regulation obedience ring and the dog given a "run-through" of the obedience exercises. Take him to a new place for each training session and give the dog the single chance he would receive at a regular trial. Corrections in strange surroundings make a dog more dependable.

Obedience exhibitors are usually called into the ring in the order their names appear in the catalog but this ruling is not compulsory. A dog may not have arrived or the owner may be busy showing a dog in another ring. But if he is available and it is his turn to compete, an exhibitor should be ready and willing to take his dog into the ring at once.

The obedience exhibitor's first act, then, after he arrives at the dog show, is to see where his dog is listed in the catalog. If among the first, the exhibitor should report his presence to the ring steward and then attend to the needs of his dog. He should exercise the dog and give him a drink of water. He should run a comb through the dog's coat or fluff his hair so he will be as proud of the dog's looks as he hopes later to be of his performance.

The majority of dogs work better when they have been left alone prior to working. In his excitement at seeing someone he knows and in his anxiety to please, the dog will perform with more enthusiasm. Instead of cuddling your dog (even the small one), fasten him on the bench or to a tree and leave him by himself for even a few moments.

Since the dog's sniffing the ground is the bane of most obedience handlers, correct your dog every time he lowers his head. Jerk up on the leash until, through repeated corrections, your dog will keep his head in the air whether he is walking around the show grounds or sitting at the ringside.

If you are not the first exhibitor at a show, stand at the ringside and watch the other handlers. Observe the pattern the judge uses for the different exercises. Plan how you can handle your dog to give him every advantage. When you work on leash, keep the leash slack. Time and time again, a dog will receive a higher score for the "off leash" exercises than he will for the "on leash," all because the owner, in his nervousness, tightened his hold on the leash.

When you enter the obedience ring, walk to one corner and make your dog sit at heel position. Await instructions from the judge, who will ask if you are familiar with the rules and if you are ready, and who will then call the commands. While waiting for the start of each exercise, keep one eye on your dog and *do not let him sniff the ground!*

During the heeling, walk briskly—do not adapt your pace to the dog's. Go in a straight line and avoid diagonal wanderings. Make your corners square and keep your about-turns smooth. In other words, work *with* your dog. When the judge asks for a "fast" or a "slow," make a distinct difference between the two paces without going to extremes. And when the judge says "Exercise finished," do not be afraid to pat and praise your dog.

Judges, as well as exhibitors, interpret the obedience rules in different ways. One point very much misunderstood among novices is that if the handler gives a second command to his dog while heeling, he fails the exercise. The rules state that only one command and/or signal may be used in obedience but in another part of the rule book it is also stated that extra commands will be penalized. Since the heeling exercises are not covered by the specific ruling that *only* one command and/or signal may be given, the novice exhibitor should not hesitate to give a second command if his dog is inattentive or temporarily distracted.

When you leave your dog by himself, such as for the sit and down stays, you can give the signal and command together. At all other times, give one or the other but not both. You can use your dog's name with a command, such as "Susie, come!" but you cannot use the dog's name when you give a signal. For instance, when you leave your dog you can signal "stay" when you give the command but you cannot say "Susie, stay!" and make a hand motion.

Little things like these may not seem important but an exhibitor can cause his dog to fail through carelessness. Study the rule book and make your home training as close to the requirements for obedience trials as possible.

In the more advanced classes, take advantage of a situation so that you do not handicap your dog by giving him too much or too little space in which to work. Use signals and commands that are distinct. There is a lot of noise and distraction at dog shows, so give your commands in a loud clear voice (without yelling) and refrain from giving a signal unless your dog is looking at you.

There are other ways you can help your dog, such as painting your dumbbell white so the dog can see it readily, or giving the dumbbell a backhand flip when you throw it, so it will not roll out of the ring. Train your dog for the unexpected so he will work under all conditions.

Disciplining a dog in public gives obedience a bad name and brings criticism of the handler. Do not punish your dog either in the obedience ring or on the dog show grounds. Give your dog a tidbit if you wish, but never in the obedience ring. The offering of food is not permissible. When you leave the ring, even though your dog is trained, snap on the leash to prevent him from running around. The unleashed dog can be a nuisance to the other exhibitors.

There will be days at dog shows when you will have all the luck of the Irish. There will be other days when the cards will seem to be stacked against you. Whether your dog passes or fails, you can make friends for obedience by letting other people know you enjoy the sport of training.

Preparing for the Dog Show

HAVING MADE up your mind to exhibit your dog, how long before the date of the show should you start getting ready? The answer, whatever the date of the show may be, is "right now." You can start with the dog's diet and conditioning, his preliminary training, and his grooming. Irrespective of any prizes you may win, you will be repaid for your efforts.

This is not the place for a dissertation upon canine nutrition, but it is not amiss to say that when a dog is fed a diet which includes a maximum of cooked or raw meat, containing some fat, he will have better physical and mental tone than if fed exclusively on canned mushes and breakfast cereals. The better grades of commercial dog foods, both in canned and cereal form, contain a high percentage of meat and when supplemented with milk, eggs, minerals, and vitamins, provide a well-balanced diet. Commercial products are easy to feed and some dogs prefer them to pure meat. The main thing is to have a strong, healthy dog and this will be evidenced by the dog's general appearance. He will be full of life, his eyes will sparkle, and his coat, whatever the length or texture, will have a live, shining quality. Only on rare occasions will the dog have such things as diarrhea or an upset stomach.

At the beginning of the conditioning process, it is well to consider whether the dog is harboring intestinal worms. A dog may have one of several varieties, some of which can be seen only through the microscope. It is suggested that at intervals of six months throughout your dog's lifetime, you take a sample of your dog's feces to your veterinarian and have him do a microscopic examination. You will then know for certain whether your dog has worms and if he has, he can be treated accordingly.

A dog with skin trouble should not be exhibited. In the first place, the dog would have trouble getting past the show veterinarian who examines each dog as he enters the show, to bar those that are sick or appear to have something contagious. And second, skin trouble is a serious handicap in that no dog can look his best unless his coat is in excellent condition. If your dog is temporarily out of coat or if he has anything wrong with his skin, consult your veterinarian. When the dog has recovered, you then can think about showing him, and chances are, you will be more successful.

Until recently, the most common parasites among dogs have been lice and fleas. Today, in some parts of the country, the American dog tick appears to lead the field. Whether you exhibit at dog shows or keep your dog as a family pet, you will want to eradicate all external parasites.

Since a dog must be over six months old to compete at a dog show, it is assumed that your dog will have been permanently inoculated against distemper and hepatitis prior to the time you plan to show him. Conscientious breeders automatically have a puppy inoculated at four or five months of age. Some breeders like the single shot method while others prefer the three shots of vaccine given at two-week intervals. If you are not familiar with either, and if your dog is still young and has not been inoculated, consult your veterinarian and follow his advice. Even an older dog or one that has been inoculated can, if he comes in contact with distemper or hepatitis, acquire it, so take extra precaution and give your dog a booster shot when he is nine months old. If you plan to take him where there are other dogs before he is nine months old, give him the booster anyway, regardless of age. The added expense will be pin money compared to what you will pay out if your dog becomes sick. If you should be so unfortunate as to lose him, you will always remember the precaution you did not take.

Exercise is another part of conditioning to think about while preparing your dog for the show ring. The amount of exercise your dog should be given will depend upon his condition at the time you begin. Do not overdo it. The dog should be brought into a moderate state of flesh, neither too fat nor too thin, without causing him to become exhausted. Merely turning the dog loose in an enclosure will not suffice unless, perhaps, you throw a ball for him to retrieve. Exercise should be regular and systematic. Daily walks on the lead bring the best results. If the walks are on city streets where the dog will meet many people, the experience will accustom him to the crowds of strangers he will be forced to endure at a dog show. Ask acquaintances to pet and handle the dog so he will become accustomed to being examined. In some shows, the dog may have to stand for as long as half an hour at a time and submit repeatedly to examination. It will be to his discredit if the dog shys or jumps away from the judge.

A vicious dog or one that is known to bite should not be in competition. During the judging, dogs must be handled and the judge should be safe in exercising his duties. As the owner, responsible for your dog's behavior, you should not show your dog unless you can trust him to behave toward strangers. If it is a question of teaching the dog to accept examination, you can force him to tolerate handling by strangers even though he may not like it, but not if the dog is a biter and attacks without warning. If you have a dog whose disposition is questionable, give him a course of obedience training and you will determine very quickly how he will react toward strangers.

To give your dog every advantage, make use of the exercise periods to teach your dog proper show ring manners. If he is inclined to pull on the leash, correct him! Jerk the leash sharply and do not move forward until the dog will walk on a slack leash. Carry pieces of food of which the dog is particularly fond, and now and then stop and either pose him or manipulate the leash until the dog assumes the position you want. When he obeys, give him his reward. Gait the dog by keeping him trotting in a brisk manner and *do not let him sniff the ground!* The dog with style and alertness frequently wins over the dog with superior body structure but atrocious manners.

Perhaps you have made a vow *never* to confine your pet in a dog crate. If you have, you are taking the wrong attitude. Sometime it may be necessary to crate your dog, so it is well to prepare him for the contingency. A regulation shipping crate, if you have room for it in the car, provides a convenient and comfortable bed for the dog when he is away from home. You will find it especially useful if you are staying with friends. A crate is a place you can leave your dog in safety, and by nailing a piece of rubber matting on the top, you will have an ideal grooming table for your convenience in preparing the dog for the ring. Start by confining the dog in the crate at home for increasingly longer periods of time. Feed him in the crate occasionally. Then, if it becomes necessary to ship your dog or to leave him in a crate over night, he will not find the confinement disagreeable.

A little more advice! Train your dog to walk up and down stairs. And even more important, take him riding to accustom him to long trips. There is nothing more discouraging than to arrive at a show with a dog that has been carsick and has drooled until he is soaking wet. The dog will not show to advantage for he will not feel up to par. Also, you will have the disagreeable job of drying him and getting his coat in shape in a limited time and without conveniences. Until the dog proves he is a good traveler, pin a bath towel around his neck (use large safety pins to fasten it) and line his crate with newspapers. Feed lightly before a trip and, in stubborn cases, give a sedative. A dog usually gets sick because he is nervous and tense. If you can help him relax, the dog will feel better and you will get more enjoyment from attending dog shows.

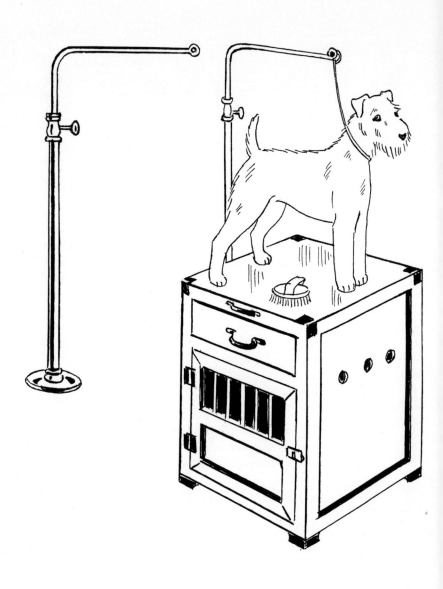

Attachable Grooming Rod

36

Grooming

ALL DOGS should be groomed regularly, but if you plan to enter your dog in a show, you will have to give more care than usual to his coat. With some breeds, such as Terriers and Poodles, it is necessary to start months in advance to get the coat in prime condition by show-time. To keep the coat looking the way it should, the dog will have to be limited in his activities. Swimming in salt water, running through the woods, and playing with other dogs will be on the list of things the dog cannot do, but he will still have fun because of the extra attention he will receive while being shown.

In order to groom a dog for the show ring, you must have a mental picture of the ideal appearance of a member of the particular breed. To work toward the attainment of that ideal, you must also have definite knowledge as to the correct method of using the tools and equipment necessary for grooming your dog. Included in this book are instructions prepared by experts in their fields, describing the proper way to groom the various breeds. In addition, there are lists of the specific tools required.

Before you start grooming your dog, study the instructions that apply to his particular breed, then consult them frequently during the grooming process in order that you may keep in mind the end result you seek to attain.

37

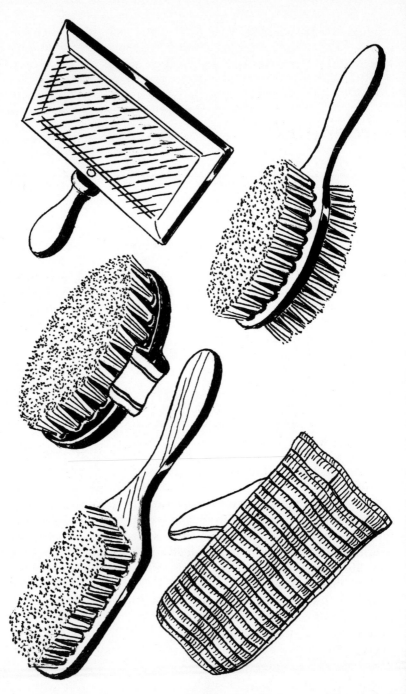

Brushes

Whatever the kind of dog to be groomed, it is essential to have the correct equipment and to know how to use it. For a single dog, the equipment need not be elaborate and it will vary somewhat from breed to breed.

First of all, you must have the right type table on which to work, placed where the hair and debris can be easily cleaned up. The top of the table must be large enough so that the dog will have no fear of falling off and does not crouch in terror. The table must have sound legs so it does not wobble and disturb either you or the dog. The height of the table should be such that it is necessary neither for you to stoop nor to reach uncomfortably high.

Professional handlers have tables of adjustable heights to be raised or lowered as the size of the dog may necessitate. The amateur can improvise a table from boards with two-by-fours as legs, or a sound old-fashioned kitchen table may serve his purpose.

A large mirror hung a few feet from the table and at a height so you may see your dog's reflection in it while you work will be of help. In trimming the dog you will be unable to look at the dog as a whole, but will see only the particular part on which you are working. An occasional glance into the mirror will enable you to see the entire dog and to work toward a total symmetry.

At intervals permit the dog to get down and run about for a few minutes. This not only will give the dog a rest and you a rest, but also will enable you to study the dog and see in perspective what you have done and how you are progressing.

Various implements and brushes are needed, their number and type depending on the breed to be groomed. But the following will be useful for any breed: dental tools for scraping accumulated tartar from the dog's teeth; clippers and files for toe nails; sharp scissors with blunted points; a dog dresser of the type that accommodates a safety razor blade; combs; a good dandy brush; a wire hound glove or wool carder; a fiber hound glove; and a supply of cloths or towels. For dogs that require barbering of the coat, the following will also be needed: hair clippers, manual or elec-

39

tric; thinning shears; and at least two stripping combs of different sizes.

Assuming that the dog to be exhibited has been brought into perfect health, that his flesh is firm and hard, that he is free from internal and external parasites, the grooming of the dog may be begun.

The feet of the dog should be inspected and if necessary the nails should be shortened. Some dogs wear their nails down with exercise, others do not. The nails of the Chihuahua should be, according to the Standard of the breed, "moderately long," which to some judges means very long. At least the Chihuahua will not be penalized for having long nails. However, the nails of all other breeds should be kept short, the shorter and stubbier the better. Long nails not only make the paws look longer than they are but also alter the shape of the foot and cause the toes to spread. The method to be used in shortening the nails is optional. Nail clippers and a file may be used, or the nails may be shortened by filing alone. If the first method is used, remove the dead part of the nail with the clippers, but not so closely as to cut into the quick and cause the nail to bleed. Using a four-way bastard file (available at any pet supply store), round the sharp edges by filing toward the end of the nail. If you prefer to perform the entire operation with files, start by filing the nail with a downward stroke (in the direction of the arrow in figure A) until the nail assumes the shape illustrated in figure B, the shaded portion being the part removed. A three-cornered file should then be used on the underside of the nail, just missing the quick, as illustrated in figure C. The operation is then complete. The dog's running about will wear the nails smooth and to the proper shape. When the nails are filed regularly, the quick gradually recedes and over a period of time the nails will shorten.

The teeth should have all accumulated tartar scraped off with dental instruments made for this purpose. If you cannot find the right tools at a pet supply store, ask your own dentist to supply you and order more than one style. The

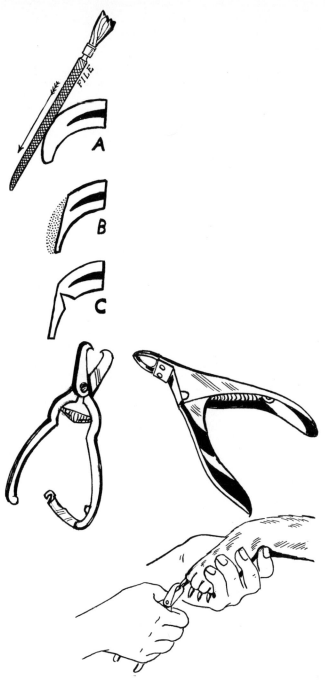

Clipping the Nails

41

broad, hook-shaped type is the most practical, but you will find a use for the other kind as well. In scraping the teeth, care must be exercised to avoid injuring the gums. Once the tartar has been removed, it is usually a simple matter to keep the teeth clean by washing them every week with cotton dipped in a moistened mixture of salt and baking soda. This will eliminate the offensive mouth odors which result from heavily encrusted teeth and infected gums.

Give special attention to the dog's ears. Some long-eared breeds are prone to ear trouble and unless the hair and wax are removed at regular intervals, serious infection may result. Dip cotton in alcohol or ether, then wrap the piece of cotton around your finger and remove the excess wax. Dust a little disinfectant powder, such as B. F. I., into the ear and with tweezers remove the dead hair. If the ear looks red and sore, squeeze in some ear ointment and check the ear again in two or three days. If at any time the dog objects to your examining his ears, repeatedly tries to scratch them, or shows other evidence of ear discomfort, it will be well to consult a veterinarian rather than to overlook the possibility of infection.

While bathing the dog must be a part of the regular routine, there can be no set rule as to how often a dog should be bathed. The color of the dog's coat and the texture of the hair are factors to consider in determining the frequency of baths. Obviously, it is essential that the dog's skin and coat be kept clean, but frequent soap and water baths may tend to soften a coat which should be wiry and also to rob the coat of its natural sheen. It may be preferable to use one of the "dry cleaner" preparations especially good for keeping show dogs in good coat. A product of this sort minimizes the task of bathing a large dog or one with a heavy coat, but even more important, it leaves no soap film. As a result, the coat looks shiny and the hair itself appears to have better texture. Dog owners would do well to inquire at pet supply stores as to the availability of such a product.

The dog should never be bathed immediately before he is to be entered in a show. With dogs that require extensive clipping, plucking, or stripping, it is well to establish the

Combs

coat pattern, then bathe the dog, after which the grooming of the coat may be completed or the pattern touched up as necessary.

Immediately before giving the bath, all mats or snarls must be removed from the coat, and throughout the bath, care must be exercise to avoid tangling the hair of the coat.

There is little to say about giving a bath to a dog, except that he should be placed in a tub of warm (not hot) water and scrubbed thoroughly. The water must be tepid, so as not to shock or chill the dog. A bland, unmedicated dog soap is best, for it will not irritate the skin or dry out the hair. Powdered detergents, marketed especially for bathing dogs, rinse away better and more easily than soap and do not leave the coat gummy or sticky. However, it is imperative that detergents be dissolved completely before they are applied to the coat and they must be used in very small amounts. Excessive amounts bleach the coat and make it dry and brittle. A few drops of disinfectant may be added to the water to discourage lice and fleas, and mineral or castor oil may be added to improve a dry skin.

It is best to begin with the interior of the ear canals, which should be cleansed thoroughly so that they not only look clean but also until no unpleasant odor comes from them. Special attention should be given to drying the ears, for many types of ear infection arise from failure to dry the canals completely. Once the ears are dried, they should be plugged with cotton to keep them free of water.

The face should be washed briskly with a cloth, but first a drop of castor oil should be placed in the eyes to protect them from soap and disinfectants. In addition, care should be taken that the cleaning solvent does not get into the dog's eyes, not because of the likelihood of causing permanent harm, but because such an experience is unpleasant to the dog and prone to prejudice him against future baths.

With the head bathed and rinsed and the surplus water removed with a towel, the body must be soaked with water, either with a hose or by dipping the water and pouring it over the dog's back until he is totally wetted. Thereafter, the soap should be applied and rubbed until it lathers freely.

44

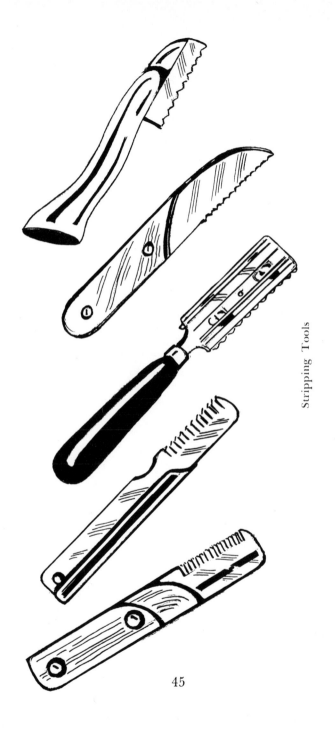

Stripping Tools

45

For some breeds a stiff brush is useful in penetrating the coat and cleansing the skin, but woolly coats should be washed by squeezing the suds through the hair. It is not sufficient to wash only the back and sides—the belly, neck, legs, feet, and tail must all be scrubbed.

If the dog's coat is very soiled, it may be well to rinse lightly and then repeat the sudsing process and scrub again. Thereafter, the dog must be rinsed with warm (tepid) water until all suds and soil come away. Lemon juice may be added to the rinse water to ensure the removal of all soap film, but its use is optional. If a bath spray is available, the rinsing is an easy matter. If the dog must be rinsed in standing water, renew it two or three times.

When the dog is thoroughly rinsed, it is well to remove from his coat such surplus water as may be squeezed with the hand, after which the dog should be enveloped in a turkish towel and lifted from the tub. In breeds such as the English Setter, which have flat lying coats, the hair may be dried until it is only slightly damp, then brushed lightly into place and set by pinning a towel around the dog's body, with one pin under the neck and another under the loin. This will lay the coat and facilitate future grooming.

With other breeds, the coat may be rubbed dry or dried with an electric hair dryer. In drying the coat, care must be exercised to avoid snarling it. If mats are formed inadvertently, they should be pulled apart gently with the fingers. In the process of drying the dog, it is well to return again and again to the interior of the ears to make sure that no dampness remains in the ear canal.

It goes without saying, of course, that the dog should not be permitted to become chilled during the bathing or drying processes. And when the coat is completely dry, it should be combed and brushed into place, after which the grooming for the show ring may be completed.

By following a regular program of grooming, you may, for a comparatively long period of time, keep the dog ready for exhibition. When the dog's coat does need more extensive grooming, there will be no need to spend weeks or months in preliminary coat conditioning.

46

In dog show parlance, the terms barbering, grooming, or coat conditioning take the form of trimming, clipping, stripping, or plucking. The extent to which any of these operations may be applicable depends largely upon the breed involved. While the primary purpose of all these operations is to remove the dead hairs of the old coat, an almost equally important objective is to establish the coat pattern dictated by the Standard for the particular breed. Today, some of the coat patterns essential in breed ring competition may appear to be the arbitrary dictates of fashion. In most instances, however, the accepted coat patterns have evolved from purely utilitarian considerations. The Poodle, dandy of the canine world, whose grooming is a tonsorial masterpiece, came by his coat pattern through the effort to increase his practicality as a hunting dog. The Poodle was in the beginning a kind of water Spaniel—his very name coming from the word "puddle." The custom of clipping arose because the dog's heavy coat hampered the use of his hindquarters in swimming. The fore part of the coat was left on as a protective jacket while the rear portions were removed to facilitate the dog's action in the water.

When the Poodle came into the drawing room, the convention of clipping his handquarters was retained, not only retained but also elaborated. We cannot pretend that the present clipping of the Poodle serves its original purposes. The Poodle is as good a water retriever as ever, but not one in a thousand is used for hunting.

Even though the accepted coat style for your breed may seem to you an unnecessary artifice, you must conform to the specified pattern if you exhibit your dog in the breed ring. For the obedience ring, more latitude is allowed in the grooming of the coat, but your dog should always be kept in such condition as to inspire in you a justifiable pride of ownership.

In clipping the Poodle, small animal clippers are preferable. Some types of clippers have detachable heads which facilitate the changing of blades. Most clippers are designed to follow the contour of the body and should be held with the clipper head flat against the dog's body, not tilted

47

on edge. To cut between the toes and along the edges of the lips, a corner of the blade should be used, for there will then be less likelihood of cutting the skin. Never use the clippers (or any other tools, for that matter) near the genitals without placing one hand to protect them. Serious injury may result if the grooming tools are used carelessly in these areas.

Furrows in the coat may result if the clippers are forced through the hair with too much pressure. Clipper burns (irritations of the skin) may also result from forcing the clippers, or from stretching the skin while clipping (the lips are an exception), using a fine blade while the skin is sensitive, or using a dull blade.

In selecting blades for the clippers, keep in mind the fact that the blades are numbered according to the closeness with which they cut—the higher the number the closer the clip. For example: No. 5 leaves the hair one-half inch long; No. 7 leaves a covering of a quarter to one-half inch; No. 10 leaves enough hair to show the natural color of the coat; No. 15 cuts closer than No. 10 and the two together, with No. 5 for winter, are all-round general purpose blades; No. 30 gives a shaved appearance. Another system of numbering clipper blades uses the single, the double, or the triple 0 sign. Again, the more numbers, the finer the clip: 0 (coarse) size leaves about the same amount of hair as the No. 5 or No. 7 blade; 00 (medium) size leaves the equal of No. 10 or longer; 000 (fine) size cuts close, as do No. 15 and No. 30.

Scissors for trimming around the ears, eyes, muzzle, or feet must be sharp but should have blunted points. There will then be less likelihood of injuring the dog if he moves unexpectedly. In scissoring any long hair of the body coat, hold the scissors in one hand and the comb in the other. Alternate combing with snipping. Comb the hair the way it falls naturally and scissor along the cut edges. Comb the hair against the natural growth and remove any overlapping hair or blend into other body length.

Thinning shears are necessary for grooming many breeds. The type having one blade smooth and the other serrated

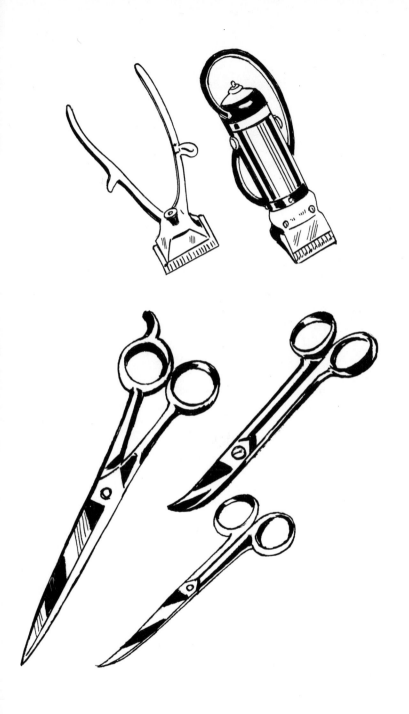

are recommended since they remove less hair and the operator is less likely to overdo the thinning. Thinning shears should be inserted well under the surface of the coat to avoid destroying the color tone of coats in which the undercoat and outer coat are different shades. Indiscriminate use of the thinning shears may accentuate faults of structure, so caution must be exercised in thinning the coat.

An oblong tool with a short handle, the carder, has bent wire teeth which are close together. It is excellent for removing mats and loosening the hair to facilitate brushing and combing.

The rake may have a single row of metal teeth or it may have two rows. It is designed in such a way that it will hack through mats of a badly tangled coat with little effort.

Combs are available in various styles and are made from plastic, bone, or metal. Since the comb should be run completely through the coat with the teeth of the comb pressing against the dog's skin, it is imperative that dog combs have rounded teeth. The length of the teeth and their distance apart will depend upon the type of coat to be groomed.

The type of coat is also the determining factor in the selection of brushes. Many kinds are available—bristles may be short or long, set in rubber or plastic backing, and may be natural pig bristles, synthetic bristles, or soft wire bristles. When brushing smooth-coated breeds, the hair should always be brushed away from the head and toward the tail. But if the coat is intended to stand away from the body, the hair should be brushed against the natural growth.

Hound gloves are available with hair, wire, or fiber bristles, and are used for removing the undercoat or for settling the outer coat and giving the final polish. The type selected depends upon the purpose it is to serve and the breed on which it is to be used.

In stripping the coat, the hair should be pulled out, not cut off. Therefore, a stripping comb with serrated teeth is more easily used than a stripping tool having a sharp, smooth, razor-like blade. Various types are available and are marketed under a variety of names. Whatever the type selected, it must be emphasized that the purpose is to pull

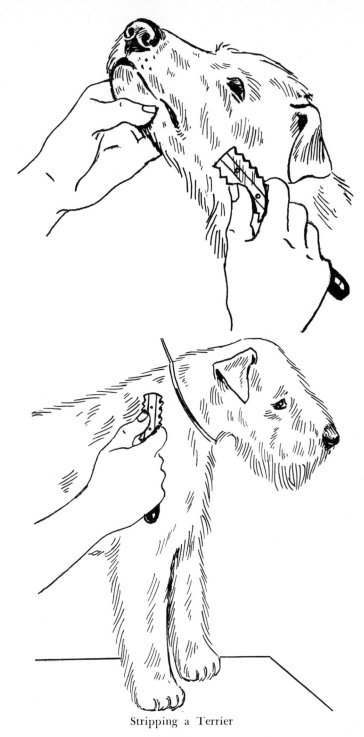

Stripping a Terrier

out the dead hairs of the coat, not to cut off the ends of healthy, live hairs securely attached to the skin. In using the stripping comb, the blade rests on the forefinger and a few hairs at a time are grasped between the blade and the thumb. If the coat is "blown" and ready to come out, it should pull easily, and the nicks on the edge of the comb will prevent taking too much hair at one time.

For plucking the coat, no tools are required. A small amount of hair is grasped between the thumb and forefinger and pulled out. While plucking is somewhat more difficult to accomplish, it gives a smoother, more even effect than does stripping and is usually the method of choice. Chalk may be used to give a firmer grip on the hair and thus make the plucking easier.

Hand rubbing, recommended for many breeds, produces a glowing coat. During the hand rubbing, any dead hairs will be uncovered and can be carefully plucked out.

It is difficult to find a conditioner of long-haired breeds who does not sing the praises of some lotion, salve, or so-called hair-grower for rubbing into the dog's skin and coat. Most such preparations are harmless, just as they are use-less. Hair is grown from the inside and most of the prepara-tions applied to a dog's skin (except those used to destroy external parasites) are wasted.

The ability to grow hair is bred into a dog, an inheritance from his ancestors. If he does not possess that inborn attri-bute, no amount or kind of food applied to his inside and no unguents or ointments rubbed into his outside will con-tribute to a further growth of hair than he was endowed with an ability to produce. However, correct and adequate nutrition will enable the clean and healthy skin to produce the live, lustrous coat the individual dog and breed is capa-ble of growing.

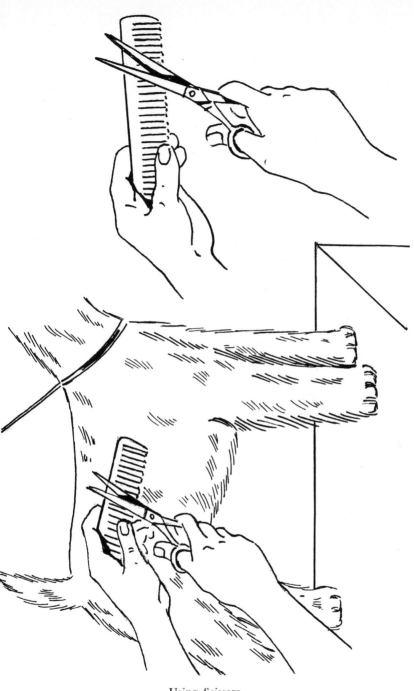

Using Scissors

Smooth-Coated Breeds

THE GENERAL BELIEF that nothing can be done to improve the appearance of smooth-coated dogs is a fallacy. Nevertheless, it is better to leave them alone than to hack, nick, gouge, or skin them, for errors in trimming are even more likely to be apparent upon smooth dogs than upon longer coated ones.

If the smooth-coated dog is to be trimmed at all, the effect should be tried well in advance for the time the dog is to be shown, in order that any errors of judgment may be rectified through a further growth of hair.

In grooming any breed, hair that is taken off must be removed for a reason—to produce a desirable effect. There should be no barbering merely for the sake of barbering. You should know the effect you want to produce, know your breed, visualize to yourself what a perfect specimen of the breed should look like. It is not always possible to achieve the effect desired, but usually a dog can be made to appear better than he actually is from a structural standpoint.

Each dog is different from every other dog. Not only is his coat different, but his structure is different. Trimming his coat does not actually change his skeleton, of course, but just how much hair is taken off and where it is taken off, and especially where it is left on, alters the animal's apparent proportions. It may be an optical illusion, but it affects what the judge sees, or at least what he thinks he sees.

A fringe of hair on the front of the neck and/or on the rear of the buttocks, thighs, or legs causes the dog to appear longer than he is, and in most breeds shortness of body is desirable. Long hair on the cheeks makes the skull look wider. Fringe over the brisket makes the body look deeper, but it also causes the legs to appear shorter. Removing the hair along the loin accentuates whatever tuck-up the dog may have, and it should be taken off or not only accordingly as the appearance of the tuck-up is desired.

The tail is sometimes improved by fining of the hair and the removal of any appearance of a brush. This statement does not apply to Beagles, Foxhounds, Bloodhounds, and Harriers, which should be permitted to carry all the brush they grow. Nor should the Smooth Fox Terrier have the hair removed to the extent of leaving him with a so-called pipe-stopper tail.

The long, coarse hairs on the muzzle, often called the feelers, should be cut off with small scissors. This may be done on the very day of the show itself, if necessary. And as with the long-coated breeds that require more extensive grooming programs, the smooth-coated breeds should have any accumulation of tartar removed from the teeth; the nails (except in the case of the Chihuahua) should be clipped; and the dog should be scrubbed to immaculate cleanliness. Then, when the coat is brushed to shining sleekness, the smooth-coated dog may be considered to be in top show-ring condition.

Long-haired Breeds

Requiring Little Trimming

COLLIES, POMERANIANS, SAMOYEDS, OLD ENGLISH
SHEEPDOGS, KEESHONDEN, SHETLAND SHEEP-
DOGS, ESKIMOS, CHOW CHOWS, GERMAN SHEP-
HERD DOGS, BELGIAN SHEEPDOGS, AND SIMILAR
BREEDS.

The dogs of the breeds named above, with a few exceptions as may be noted, require no trimming. They do need
bathing and extensive combing and brushing. The hard
whiskers on the foreface, the feelers, when they are visible,
may be nipped off with sharp scissors having blunted points.
When working around the muzzle, press the upper and
lower jaws firmly together to avoid injuring the tongue or
the lips.

Collies, Poms, and Shelties should have ears as small as
possible. Many times fringes grow on the edges of the ears,
causing them to appear larger than they are. Those fringes
should be removed, but care must be taken that the ears
do not look hacked or tampered with. The stripping comb
may be used for this purpose, grasping the protruding hairs
between the comb and the ball of the thumb and pulling
out (*not cutting off*) the excess fringes. Scissors may also
be used, but if they are, caution must be exercised to prevent
nicks. In a few days the growing hair will cover tiny nicks.

Coats of German Shepherd Dogs and Belgian Sheepdogs should be brushed flat. Constant and frequent brushing is all that is required. The hound glove is useful in flattening such coats, but in using it care must be employed not to pull out the undercoat characteristic of the breeds. The undercoat is a protection to the skin and provides a cushion for the outer coat. While the coats of German Shepherd Dogs and Belgian Sheepdogs are brushed flat, the undercoat prevents the outer coat from hugging the body as it would in a single-coated animal.

A comb with extremely fine teeth, such as one with which fleas are removed, is also prone to tear out the undercoat. A coarse comb, however, can well be used as a preliminary to the brushing. The brushing is to be followed with a good dressing down with the hound glove.

If the grooming is begun several months before the German Shepherd Dog or the Belgian Sheepdog is to be exhibited, there is no harm and possibly some benefit in tearing out the loose part of the undercoat with the hound glove. The skin, of course, should not be irritated in the process. The outer coat, with the undercoat removed, will cling too tightly to the skin at first. But the undercoat will grow again and will be firmly attached to the skin. It should be well raked out with the hound glove at intervals of several months, but should never be taken out just before a show.

The Old English Sheepdog should have preserved every hair that it is possible to keep. No hair except that which is loose should be combed or brushed from him. Care must also be taken not to break the coat.

All snarls should be removed gently with a coarse comb. The brush should be employed daily, but no hair pulled out by the roots. After brushing it flat, loosen the coat again, using the coarse-toothed comb. The coat should not stand off, brushed the wrong way of its grain, as does the Collie coat, but it should not cling to the dog's skin. Rather, the coat should be loosened with the comb to achieve the effect of a big, loosely lying coat.

Talcum powder sprinkled profusely into such a coat and

then carefully and completely brushed out helps to bring about the correct appearance. The long hair of the brow should be combed forward over the face even to the point of obscuring the eyes.

The hair of the legs and feet should be as profuse as possible. The Old English Sheepdog is left actually smothered in hair—the more of it the better. Many a heavily coated one has won over another of better structure just on the strength of a superb and spectacular jacket.

Such breeds as Old English Sheepdogs sometimes come into the ring with so much powder in their coats as to emit a cloud of dust when they are touched. While its use is seldom penalized by judges, it renders the dog and his handler ridiculous. If talcum powder is employed at all, it should be so thoroughly brushed out of the coat as not to blow off the dog or even to rub off on clothing.

Collies, Pomeranians, Shetland Sheepdogs, Samoyeds, Keeshonden, Eskimos, and Chow Chows are exhibited with their hair standing out from their bodies. In the course of grooming these breeds, it is necessary to brush the coats with the grain as well as against it, but in the final grooming before the dog goes into the ring, the coat should be forced to stand up as much as possible. Therefore, the final brushing should be against the grain.

Many amateurs believe that these breeds should possess soft, down-like hair. Nothing could be further removed from the truth. Their undercoats are indeed soft and oily, but the guard hairs of the outer coat are harsh and bristly. The crisper and harder the outer coat, the better will it stand off when brushed to do so. The thicker and denser the undercoat, the better will it support the coarser hairs of the outer coat when brushed to stand away.

Gilder's whiting (pure white chalk) rubed into the thoroughly dampened coat and permitted to dry completely gives the coat an added crispness and acts as a starch to cause the coat to stand off when brushed to stand up during the final stages of drying. The brushing of the dried whiting from the coat is, however, a serious chore. It requires brushing and brushing and brushing. Unless the last traces of whiting are removed, it can be seen, especially in a colored coat, and, what is even worse, feels gritty to the hand in examination of the coat. If any whiting remains it will be apparent to the judge that it has been used and may be considered to be a kind of faking. It is not faking to use whiting provided that all traces of it are brushed out.

On colored dogs, fuller's earth is an acceptable substitute for whiting. Finer in its texture, it is not so harsh to the touch and is less noticeable to the eye than whiting. Fuller's earth, too, must be thoroughly brushed out, but if some traces remain, they are not so likely to be detected.

American Kennel Club rules forbid the use of any substance that alters a dog's appearance in the show ring. Chalk, talcum powder, etc., *must be brushed out* before entering the ring.

Kerry Blue Terrier

1. Before Trimming

2. After Trimming

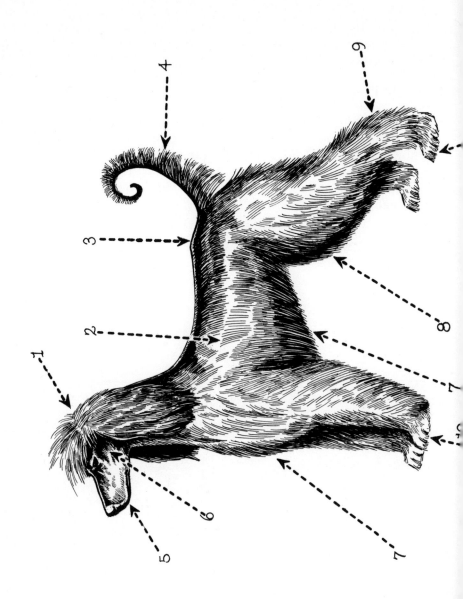

AFGHAN HOUND

1. Brush topknot forward and up (wild, not parted).
2. Pluck or strip to even up saddle line. Saddle should be naturally short on mature Hounds but not on puppies. Sandpaper may be used to clean off saddle.
3. Keep saddle wide and flat at croup, not bushy at tail set. Hip bones should appear prominent.
4. Even up feathering on tail and taper to end of tail with scissors if necessary.
5. Trim whiskers or not, as desired. Close trimming of whiskers improves appearance if head is coarse.
6. Clean off hair or fuzz on cheeks of mature dogs, accentuating length of head.
7. Brush coat down to hang like silk.* Coat should never appear matted.
8. Brush hair forward to show bend of stifle.
9. Brush hair close to emphasize low-set hock.
10. Brush hair on feet forward and to side. Clean out hair between pads.

* Soft water sprayed on coat before brushing facilitates grooming.

Tools

Long-bristled brush—whalebone bristles preferred.
Wide-toothed bone or steel comb (to be used sparingly).
Stripping comb.
Scissors with rounded points.

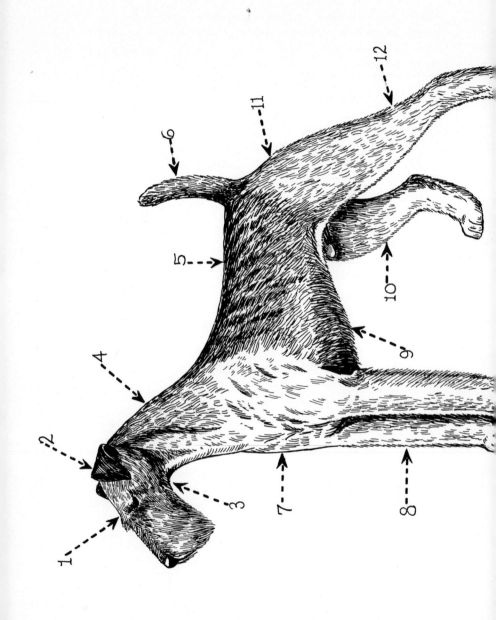

AIREDALE TERRIER

1. Trim head to appear oblong with profile flat, and also having rectangular appearance when viewed from above; trim skull closely; level hair between eyes, but not so much as to appear scooped out; thin and level eyebrows to lie almost flat—taper from very close at outer corner of eye to rather long at inside corner of eye. Clip hair of muzzle in front of eyes neatly but not too closely, making muzzle appear well filled in and powerful and keeping the eyes from being obscured. To emphasize rectangular appearance, trim hair at corner of mouth rather closely but not so far forward as to make muzzle look snipey, nor so far back as to cause an indentation of outline. Trim hair under jaw very closely to a point below corner of mouth, then taper into beard, which should be squared off. Too profuse facial furnishings should be thined, as Schnauzer trim is to be avoided.

2. Strip ears very closely.

3. Trim throat and front of neck closely.

4. Trim neck to accentuate arch, taking hair down fairly closely at base of skull, tapering into crest, and blending neatly into withers and shoulders without abrupt angle.

5. Trim back level.

6. Trim hair on tail but not too closely. Should be about same length as hair of coat and just as tight. Do not taper tail too much.

7. Strip closely on shoulders and forechest. Trim closely on upper arm, around arm to body, and under arm. Gradually taper hair of upper arm into leg furnishings at elbow.

8. Trim forelegs to appear absolutely straight from any direction. Trim forefeet closely so as to be almost hidden by furnishings. Remove hair close to pad at back of foot, and, down to that point, taper furnishings on back of pastern. Remove excess hair between pads.

9. Even up hair on chest, leaving more on leggy dogs than on cobby—ideal length being approximately level with elbows at front, then trimmed in fairly straight line diagonally to tuck-up, where hair should be taken down fairly closely. Even flank hair and blend into thigh furnishings.

10. Remove scraggly hair and trim outline to accentuate bend of stifle. Remove long hairs from inside of stifle.

11. Trim hindquarters neatly, blending coat hair into furnishings at rise of thigh muscle and tapering into flank hair. Trim fairly closely and evenly from under tail, around inside of thigh, then blend into leg furnishings.

12. Even outline of leg down to hock. Trim back pastern to appear absolutely straight when viewed from rear. Remove excess leg furnishings on outside of thigh, blend into furnishings of gaskin (second thigh) and on down to feet. Trim hair around foot and from between pads, tapering hair on back of pastern from closely at hock to fairly long, then closely again at pad, giving somewhat rounded appearance when viewed from side. Trimming hair too closely on inside of hindquarters will make dog look bowlegged, while leaving too much, too high, on outside of legs and quarters will make dog appear too close behind.

Tools

Stripping comb.
Scissors with blunted points.
Clippers.
Thinning shears.

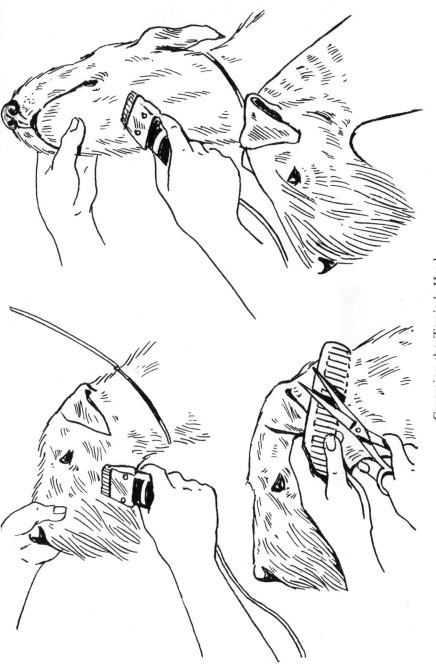

Grooming the Terrier's Head

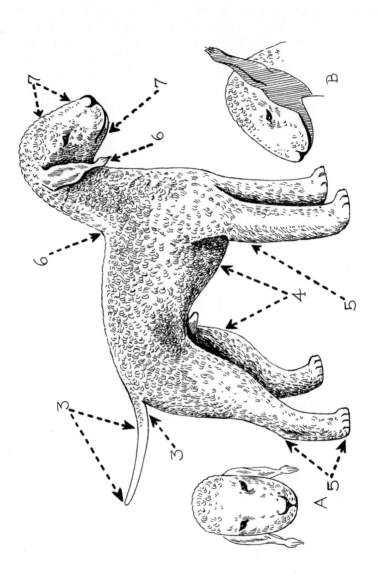

BEDLINGTON TERRIER

1. Place dog on good steady table, preferably with rubber mat on top to keep dog's feet from slipping.

2. Remove all mats and knots from coat by parting hair with left hand, then, with comb held in right hand, combing out from skin. Comb out every portion of the coat thoroughly.

3. Remove all hair from last (distal) two-thirds of tail. Trim under portion of first (proximal) third, then neatly and gradually blend top hair of tail into body hair of stern.

4. Again comb body coat. With an imaginary line on any plane of body, cut hair until length is three-fourths to one inch all over body. Then remove slightly more hair from sides of chest cage to give definite flat-sided appearance. Trim hair on loin to about one half-inch in length. Accentuate depth of brisket and tuck-up by clipping hair on abdomen as far forward as navel. Trim tuck-up neatly.

5. Comb leg hair again and begin trimming feet by evening up all hair around pads and toes. Remove all mats and discolored hair between toes. Even hair on rest of leg, being sure not to leave any tufts on elbow and hock.

6. Trim hair on throat very closely, gradually blending into somewhat longer hair on sides of neck and longest on nape where hair blends into that of shoulders and back line.

7. Emphasize topknot by clipping very closely between eye and ear (upper portion of shaded area in illustration), then rounding topknot from ear to ear in graceful, eye-catching curve. Locate Adam's apple, then with clippers clip a strip from just above Adam's apple right up to lower lip. With scissors, blend longest chest hair into base of clipped area at so-called "apple line." Extend clipped area in parallel strips to corners of mouth. With scissors cut off all hair around lower lip and any hairs that hang over edges of upper lip. Ex-

tend clipped area up over cheeks and sides of head. Do not clip above line extending from upper front edge of ear to outer corner of eye. *Do not* remove hair around eye, for the Bedlington should have a small, well-sunken eye which is never prominent; the eyebrow helps give this appearance. Clip ear closely inside and out, taking care not to go above little mass of cartilage at upper boundary of ear. Tassel is formed by long hair left on last inch or so at tip of ear. Finish side edges of ear with scissors, taking care not to injure folds of skin at back edge of ear.

Amount of hair left on muzzle depends on width of skull between ears and at cheeks. Thicker head will require more hair on muzzle than will cleaner (leaner) head. When viewed from front, head should have appearance of blunt wedge, with muzzle only slightly narrower than skull. Head should look smoothly trimmed from any and all angles. Make doubly certain there are no tufts anywhere on head, look for any long hairs and remove them. Nothing should spoil smooth curves of head. The line of the topknot should rise from the nose and arch gracefully over the high point at the occiput, then blend neatly into the arched neck with no break in line. In trimming the head, it is well to view the Bedlington against a dark background.

Tools

Sharp scissors with blunted points.
Strong comb—metal or plastic.
Clippers with No. 000 blades.
Block of whiting or chalk.

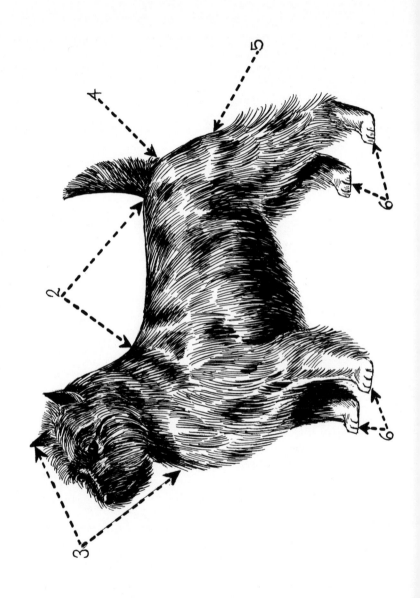

CAIRN TERRIER

1. Brush and comb coat thoroughly to remove matted or loose hair and any surface soil. Outer coat of Cairn Terrier should be harsh and weather resisting; undercoat, short, soft, and furry.

2. Check general outline of dog. Level top line by plucking loose hair or removing with stripping comb (fine blade).

3. Check outline of furnishings on head, plucking out any long straggling hairs that spoil line of ruff. Head furnishings should be plentiful. Clean tips of ears outside and inside either by plucking or with stripping comb. Make clean line around edges of ears with straight scissors.

4. Plucking with fingers or using stripping comb, take hair off back of tail, shaping so that tail is thick at base then tapers to a point at tip.

5. Comb hair well down over hindquarters. Remove any straggly hair either by plucking or stripping so that coat will lie smoothly over hindquarters.

6. Remove any long hairs around feet by plucking or stripping, then with straight scissors trim neatly around front of feet.

Tools

Stripping comb (optional).
Scissors with blunted points.

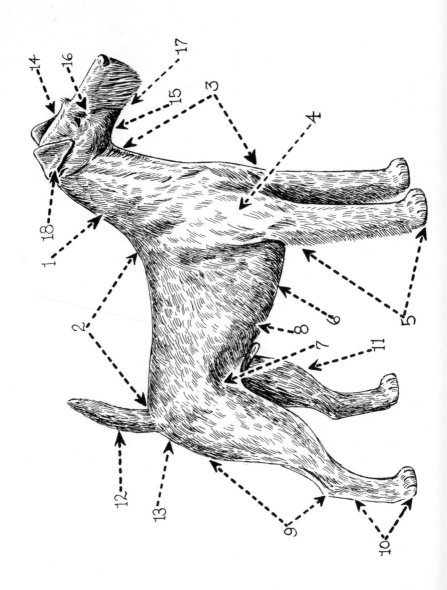

IRISH TERRIER

1. Trim hair on neck very closely and evenly, tapering gradually into withers (the point of the shoulders).

2. Trim the back from withers to tail-set evenly but not as closely as neck. Leave hair about one-half to three-fourths inch long.

3. Trim front part of neck and brisket closely, leaving on just a shade more hair as you work down, until you reach point where front legs join body; taper hair lengths from neck to forelegs so there are no breaks in evenness of hair line.

4. Trim front shoulders evenly and closely. Be sure not to leave any holes either at top of shoulder or below where shoulder joins upper leg.

5. Trim hair on front legs evenly to straighten leg lines. Trim principally the hair on back of front legs. Trim superfluous hair from between toes and from edges of feet, shaping to neat roundness.

6. Shape rib cage to follow body conformation from the short, fine hair on back to a fuller coat on under part of ribs and chest. On sides and under chest do not leave long hair that is in any way discolored or shaggy.

7. Trim loin so as not to emphasize tuck-up.

8. Trim all shaggy or snarled hair from belly, then even hair length.

9. Trim thighs from back line to hocks, taking off sufficient hair to show definite outline of stifle joint in front and hock joint behind.

10. Straighten rear line of hock and trim superfluous hair from between toes and from edges of hind feet to shape to neat roundness.

11. Trim insides of hind legs down to hock joint to give ample room to visualize movement.

12. Trim tail evenly, though not too closely, to a tip.

13. Trim stern evenly and closely.

14. Trim skull very closely. Even the eyebrow hair. Leave slightly more hair over inside corner of eye than outside to emphasize expression.

15. Trim cheeks clean from corners of mouth back to neck line.

16. Trim under eyes to emphasize expression.

17. Clean under jaw from corners of mouth back to neck line. Leave chin whiskers and beard, and brush forward. Even front of beard.

18. Clean off ears, inside and out, straighten edges with scissors. Pull out long hairs in ear canal.

Tools

Scissors with blunted points.
Clippers.
Stripping comb.

CARE OF FEET

All Irish Terriers are subject to cracked or horny pads. Remove loosened horns and edges with scissors, taking care not to cut into live flesh.

Thoroughly massaging pads with lubricant such as olive oil, etc., is helpful in correcting this condition. Dog should not be exercised on rough surfaces while pads are sore.

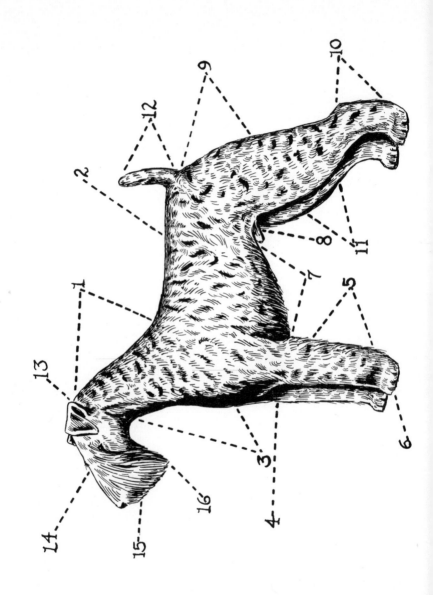

KERRY BLUE TERRIER

In grooming the Kerry, begin by cleaning coat without pulling out too much hair. Remove knots or mats. Use "slicker" held tightly in one hand while small area of hair is separated by other hand.

Be careful not to leave deep scissors marks by cutting too much hair at once. Particular care must be exercised in trimming neck and shoulders so that hair of each blends into other without a break in the desired smooth line.

1. Blend from short hair of occiput to long hair of withers.
2. Straighten top line of coat, leaving hair about one and one-half to two inches in length. Comb body coat from front to rear.
3. Clean brisket from under part of neck to lower part of brisket.
4. Clean so depth of chest is visible.
5. Trim long dead hair with scissors so leg hair is even all around. Comb leg hair down.
6. With scissors, trim long hair from between toes and pads. Shape forefeet to neat roundness.
7. Taper underline of chest gently. Remove hair cleanly around organs.
8. Trim hair to about three-quarters to one inch in length to accentuate tuck-up.
9. Strip rump hair short.
10. Trim with scissors to show let-down hocks. Comb leg hair down.
11. Trim to show bend of stifle.
12. Strip, then with scissors trim straight. Take care not to cut dip into back line when tail is carried gaily or slightly down.

13. Clean top of head, cheeks, ears, and underneath ears. Straighten edges of ears with scissors. In trimming ears, take care that double fold is not cut or lacerated.

14. Allow brow to cover eye. Comb forward to blend with beard.

15. With scissors, even length of beard, removing discolored dead ends.

16. Blend from beard to cheek.

Tools

Wide-toothed comb, metal or plastic.
"Slicker."
Clippers.
Stripping comb.
Scissors with blunted points.

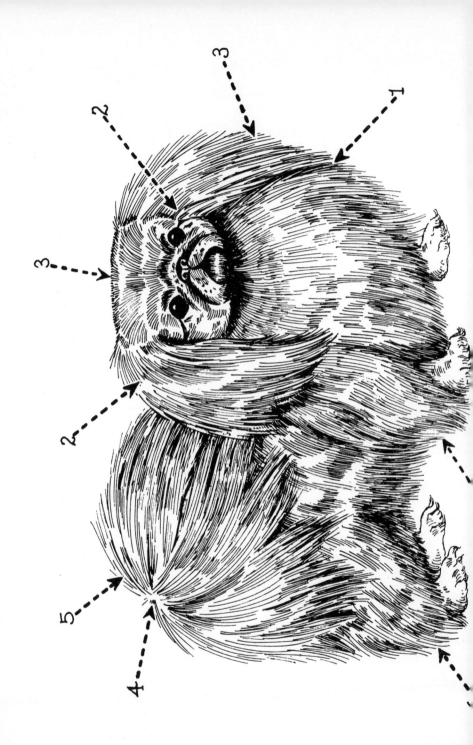

PEKINGESE

1. Brush coat up from sides to emphasize appearance of wide, heavy front.

2. Comb hair from underneath ears forward toward face.

3. Brush hair on top-skull back, giving flat, square look and avoiding apple-headed look or appearance of roundness of skull. Comb ear fringes forward to give feathery effect.

4. With brush, part hair of tail in middle, letting feathering fall to either side of body to emphasize shortness of back.

5. Use comb freely on feathering, ear fringes, tail, etc.

6. Use brush on body and undercoat.

In grooming the Pekingese, first clean off any surface grime with damp washcloth. Brush coat thoroughly, leaving no mats or knots. Dust powder through coat, working well into fringes, then brush outward from roots of hair, completely removing all powder. Pour a small amount of coat dressing into shallow vessel so that brush may be dipped in dressing. Dampen (but do not wet) coat by brushing dressing into it. Massage powder into coat again, then groom with brush as described above.

Tools

Pig-bristle brush with rubber back. Bristles should be about one and one-quarter inches long.
Steel comb with widely spaced teeth.

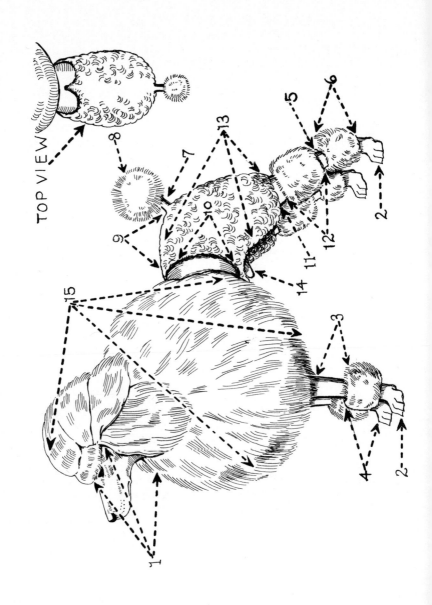

TOP VIEW

POODLE

ENGLISH SADDLE CLIP

(Accepted breed ring clip.)

1. Clip face clean. Cut from in front of ear to between eyes and to a point four or five inches down on throat. Use No. 15 blade on top of nose, under eyes, and around muzzle, but use No. 10 blade on sides of face and throat. Curve throat line to give appearance of a necklace. When working around mouth, press jaws together firmly to avoid cutting tongue.

2. Using No. 15 blade, clip feet to leave an inch or more of ankle exposed. Remove all hair between toes and pads, and trim neatly around nails.

3. Leaving two and one-half to three and one-half inches of unclipped hair above ankle, use No. 15 blade to remove all hair to the elbow, without uncovering bone itself.

4. With scissors, trim bracelet to two or more inches in length. Comb down and cut along bottom edge. Comb up and scissor along top edge. Fluff hair out and shape evenly.

5. Using No. 15 blade, cut band one to one and one-half inches wide completely around leg. Stay above hock joint.

6. Shape lower bracelet with scissors, leaving more hair at hock than at ankle.

7. Clip top side of tail toward body. Clip underside of tail away from body. Use No. 15 blade, or if skin is sensitive, No. 10. Clipped portion of tail should measure approximately three inches.

8. Comb pompon and shape with scissors. Tuft of tail should not wilt and hang down. Grow pompon back from end or extend it past tail itself to allow for improper docking.

9. Use No. 5 blade to shorten long hair on back and sides of hindquarters, but do not cut below hips or over loins. If you prefer, use scissors to reduce length of coat on hindquarters. Except for along back, leave at least two inches of hair. Separate long hair from short hair approximately at last rib. Using No. 15 blade and working toward head, cut a band one inch wide completely around body.

10. Clip the crescent shaped saddle with No. 15 blade, cutting against hair. Deepest point of crescent is in vertical line with point where rear leg joins body. When crescent is too far back, it gives impression of weak hindquarters.

11. Clip band three-fourths to one inch wide completely around back leg. Use No. 15 blade. To mark exact line first, turn clippers over and press blade, which is pointed downward, against leg. Stay below stifle joint and slope slightly toward front. After marking line, turn clippers to usual position and cut against hair to widen band and make line distinct.

12. Trim saddle bracelet with scissors. Comb down and scissor along cut edge. Comb up and do same. Fluff hair out and shape to desired length.

13. Scissor pack, leaving inch or more of hair. Shape to hindquarters, leaving them even and symmetrical. Scissor along all cut edges. With scissors or No. 5 blade, remove shaggy hair on insides of back legs.

14. Clip the stomach and penis with No. 10 blade. Cut with hair.

15. Brush the long coat. Teach your Poodle to relax when being brushed and train him to lie on his side while you do shoulders and stomach. Pay special attention to areas under ears and between front legs. Have dog sit while you brush chest. Remove all mats, first brushing them apart with fingers, and make final brushing toward head so as to make hair stand out from body. Scissor shaggy hair to leave coat even. On ears, tidy feathering but leave full. Fasten forelock back with elastic band, barrette, or ribbon. Do not scissor above eyes.

Measurements given are for Standard Poodle. For Toys and Miniatures, lines of pattern must be scaled down to fit proportions of dog. Blade numbers included in instructions are approximate. Since density of Poodle coats varies, the blade suggested may not be best for your dog. Experience will teach you which blades are best suited for your dog.

Tools

Comb.
Brush.
Clippers.
Scissors with blunted points.

NOTE: Like fashions, Poodle styles change. Present trends are: the line that separates the long coat from the saddle is kept a considerable distance in back of, and not at, the last rib; the forelegs are clipped to within one or two inches but not completely to the elbow; half-moons are made over the loins instead of bringing the saddle to a point along the spine. Still another trend, and a controversial one, is the tendency to leave heavy, bulbous packs which cause one to lose sight of the Poodle. The Standard definitely calls for a "short" blanket of hair on the hindquarters. A Poodle exhibitor should study the clips on other Poodles and then make his own deductions for improving his Poodle's appearance by changing lines and by scissoring.

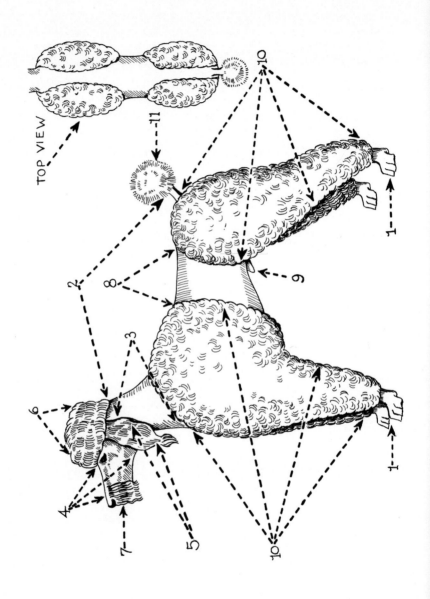

TOP VIEW

1 1 2 3 4 5 6 7 8 9 10 11

ROYAL DUTCH CLIP

(Not acceptable in American breed ring but acceptable in obedience ring.)

1. Using No. 15 blade, clip feet to leave an inch or more of ankle exposed. Remove hair between toes and pads, and trim neatly around nails. If feet are left _unclipped, scissor around paws to give compact appearance, and remove hair from between pads.

2. Clip a strip the width of the clippers from base of skull to pompon on tail, using No. 10 blade (No. 5 in winter).

3. Clip neck by extending the strip from ear to ear, working from skull toward shoulders. Clip throat *toward* muzzle, leaving circular throat line to give appearance of necklace.

4. Remove hair from face but leave whiskers, starting at corners of mouth and extending completely around muzzle. Use No. 15 blade on top of nose and under eyes, but use No. 10 blade on sides of face and on throat.

5. Using No. 15 blade, remove hair from both inside and outside of ear. Leave enough hair on tip to form tassel. Clip *toward edge* of ear, not against natural growth. Hold ear flat on palm of hand to avoid cutting ear itself. With scissors trim shaggy hair of tassels to give tidy appearance.

6. Comb topknot and shape with scissors to give rounded appearance. Shorten hair over eyes and ears, and on side of skull. Blend hair on back of neck into clipped portion of body.

7. Comb whiskers and trim them evenly. Cut hair close at corners of mouth. Shorten hair on top of nose.

8. With No. 10 blade (No. 5 in winter) make circular cut from back line to loin to form chap on leg, and from back line to underside of ribs to form front leg chap. Round to give symmetrical appearance. Remove all hair on sides and under stomach.

9. Clip penis with No. 10 blade, cutting toward end, away from body.

10. Shape chaps with scissors and even long hair after combing chaps thoroughly. If hair is extra long, remove shaggy hair on insides of back legs and along stomach, using scissors or No. 5 blade. (If No. 10 blade was used on body, clip stomach with No. 10 as well.)

11. Comb pompon and shape with scissors. Tuft of tail should not wilt and hang down. Grow pompon back from end or extend it past tail itself to allow for improper docking.

Measurements given are for Standard Poodle. For Toys and Miniatures, lines of pattern must be scaled down to fit proportions of dog. Blade numbers included in instructions are approximate. Since density of Poodle coats varies, the blade suggested may not be best for your dog. Experience will teach you which blades are best suited for your dog.

Tools

Comb.
Brush.
Clippers.
Scissors with blunted points.

PUPPY CLIP

One of the three styles accepted in the American breed ring, the Puppy Clip is for dogs under one year of age, and includes clipping of face, feet, and tail, only. The rest of the coat is left at its full length but may be tipped with scissors to remove shaggy ends. For instructions on clipping face, feet, and tail, see chart for English Saddle Clip.

CONTINENTAL CLIP

The Continental, also acceptable in the American breed ring, is a variation of the English Saddle Clip. The only difference is that all the hair is removed from the hindquarters, except for the two lower bracelets on the back legs and two rosettes, one on each hip. The rosettes are shortened to about two inches in length and rounded to look smooth and even. The pompon is left on the tail. For instructions on clipping other areas, see chart for English Saddle Clip.

SHAWL CLIP

Though still a favorite with some owners, the Shawl Clip is no longer seen frequently. Acceptable in the obedience ring but not in the American breed ring, the Shawl Clip is a variation of the English Saddle Clip or the Continental Clip, with front legs left full, and, as the name implies, gives the appearance of a large shawl draped over the shoulders.

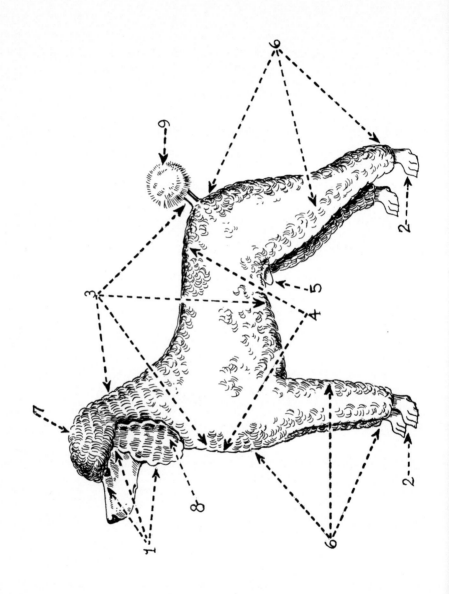

KENNEL CLIP

(Acceptable in obedience ring but not in American breed
   ring.)

1. Clip face clean. Cut from in front of ears to between
    eyes and to a point four or five inches down on throat.
    Use No. 15 blade on top of nose, under eyes, and around
    muzzle, but No. 10 blade on sides of face and on
    throat. Clip throat *away* from head to avoid distinct
    line that will make blending into body hair more diffi-
    cult. When working around mouth, press jaws to-
    gether firmly to avoid cutting tongue.

2. Using No. 15 blade, clip feet to leave inch or more of
    ankle exposed. Remove all hair from between toes
    and pads and trim neatly around nails. If feet are left
    unclipped, scissor around pads to give compact appear-
    ance, and remove hair from between pads.

3. Using No. 5 blade in winter and No. 10 blade in sum-
    mer, start at base of skull and clip toward tail. Re-
    move all hair from body, including neck, shoulders,
    ribs, and stomach, but *do not* cut below hips or shoulder
    bones. Leave at least two inches of hair over loins for
    blending.

4. Blend body length hair into leg length on hips, loins,
    shoulders, and chest. Use scissors, or, if No. 10 blade
    was used on body, No. 7 or No. 5 blade can be used
    against long hair at blending line to give smooth, even
    appearance.

5. Clip penis with No. 10 blade. Remove shaggy hairs on
    inside of back leg, using scissors or No. 15 blade.

6. Comb leg hair thoroughly and scissor to desired length of about two and one-half to three inches. If hair is excessively long, remove outer portion with No. 5 blade, holding clippers free of body. Scissor along clipped part of feet. Comb hair of legs up and scissor even. Comb hair down and scissor again. Fluff hair out from body and shape for angulation.

7. Comb topknot and shape to rounded appearance. Scissor hair over eyes and ears, and on sides of skull. Blend into body length hair on back of neck.

8. Comb hair on ears. Leaving ears full, remove shaggy hairs with scissors.

9. Comb pompon and shape with scissors. (It is optional whether tail is clipped closer than body. If No. 15 blade is used on tail, clip top side toward body and underside away from body to avoid irritating skin.) The tuft of the tail should not wilt or hang down. Grow pompon back from end or extend it past tail itself to allow for improper docking.

Measurements given are for Standard Poodle. For Toys and Miniatures, lines of pattern must be scaled down to fit proportions of dog. Blade numbers included in instructions are approximate. Since density of Poodle coats varies, the blade suggested may not be best for your dog. Experience will teach you which blades are best suited for your dog.

Tools

Comb.
Brush.
Clippers.
Scissors with blunted points.

TERRIER DUTCH CLIP

This is the Kennel Clip body with the Royal Dutch head. Poodle owners who favor a simple clip, but prefer whiskers and ear tassels to the clean face and full ears, are partial to the Terrier Dutch Clip, which is acceptable in the obedience ring but not the American breed ring.

CORDED POODLE

Corded Poodles are seldom, if ever, exhibited in American shows, and it appears futile to go into the theoretical process of maintaining such a dog. It requires a great deal of time and patience to maintain a coat that is permitted to accumulate in cords of such length that they reach to the floor. The corded effect was created by the mats of the twisted hair adhering together and the ends of the cords themselves being snarled into the live hair. In some cases the cords, which had to be oiled to keep them from breaking, grew several feet in length, making it impossible to wash the dog or to exercise him adequately.

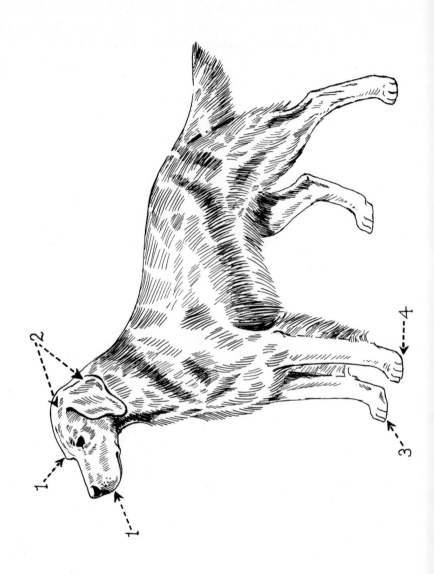

GOLDEN RETRIEVER

1. Trim away whiskers and eyebrows.

2. With thinning shears and stripping comb, remove any excess growth of hair from in front of and behind ears. Care must be exercised to give appearance of neatness, not artificiality.

3. Trim nails.

4. With scissors, trim hair around feet to emphasize tight, compact paws.

A daily brushing will prevent mats forming and keep the Golden Retriever's coat free from dead hairs.

Tools

Scissors with blunted points.
Stripping comb.
Brush.
Thinning shears.

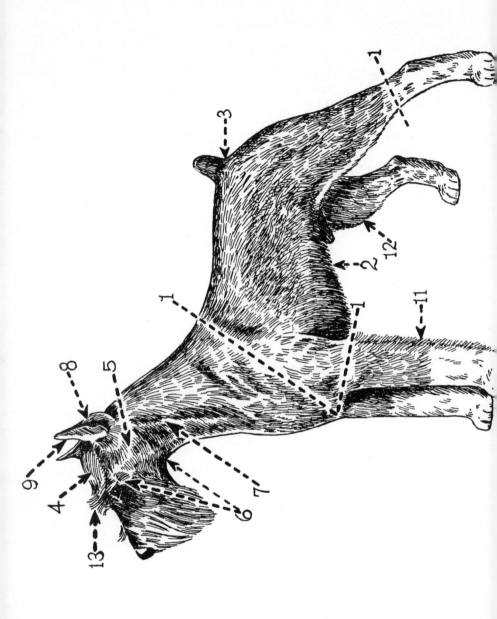

MINIATURE SCHNAUZER

1. Strip body back of line indicated, removing outer coat.

2. Remove long hairs under chest and on chest itself, shaping line to suit the particular dog.

3. Remove all long hair on tail. With scissors, clip closely on "butterfly" beneath tail. The more closely the hairs are removed here, the shorter the body will appear to be.

4. Strip or pluck closely on skull.

5. Remove hair closely on cheeks.

6. Remove long hairs and pluck or strip (as closely as possible without leaving bare spots) on area under neck, in a straight line from outer corner of eye to mouth and under throat.

7. Clean neck.

8. Strip outside of ears closely.

9. Using scissors, clip hair on inside of ears, and trim hair on edges of ears evenly.

10. Clip neatly around feet.

11. With scissors, even hair on legs to give straight line.

12. Remove long hairs on inside of thighs.

13. Even eyebrows with scissors, cutting closely at outer corner of eye, gradually curving to greatest length at inner corner. Even ends of whiskers.

The Miniature Schnauzer should be groomed regularly so that mats will not form in furnishings. In using comb and brush, care must be taken that furnishings are not pulled out. In using a stripping comb, coat must be pulled out —not cut off. Preferably, the Schnauzer coat should be groomed in successive stages. Beginning about ten weeks before show, strip body area down to undercoat. If long, the hair under chest, on chest itself, and underneath throat can be plucked at this time. Undercoat in these areas usually becomes loose in a short time and may then be plucked, also. When new coat appears on top of back, strip top of neck down to withers, also tail and "butterfly" beneath tail, and under part of throat if it was not done earlier. Head and ears should be plucked closely at regular intervals as coat begins to grow and loosen. Two or three weeks before show, hair should be removed (as closely as possible without leaving bare spots) from cheeks, neckridge, under part of throat, outside of ears, skull, stomach, and underneath tail. Final touches may be given coat a day or two before show, or on show day itself.

Tools

Stripping comb.
Metal comb.
Brush.
Scissors with blunted points.
Grooming mitten useful but not essential.

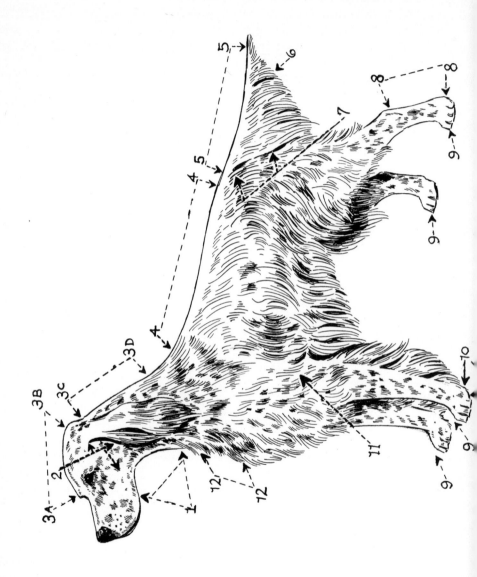

ENGLISH SETTER

1. Clip hair between arrows numbered "1." (If using coarse head, No. 5 or No. 7, trim upward against growth of hair. If using fine head, No. 10 or No. 15, trim downward with growth of hair.) Trim cleanly and evenly around throat and up to hair line under ears.

2. Clip cleanly between arrows (about one and one-half inches). Blend edges of clipped area with stripping comb. Clip excess hair from cheeks. Remove all hair under ear and long hair inside ear.

3. Remove hair in areas marked "3" with stripping comb. *Do not use clippers.* Between 3A and 3B hair should be longer than between 3C and 3D. Between 3C and 3D trim hair all around neck and down to hair line, which is under ears. Hair should be left longer as 3D is approached.

4. Between points numbered "4," trim only hair which is exceptionally unruly. Comb and brush frequently to make hair lay flat, giving better appearance than when trimmed.

5. Remove bushiness but not feathering. Also strip on either side of tail to remove bushiness.

6. Trim feathering on tail to tapered point. Strip lightly to avoid freshly cut look.

7. With stripping comb, remove very curly hair on rear, and near and under tail.

8. Removal of long hair on hock is optional but gives neater appearance. Strip, or cut with scissors not too closely but until neat look is achieved.

9. Do not remove all hairs between toes. Shorten long hairs which stick out. After nails are trimmed, cut hair between pads short. With scissors, remove long hairs covering pads when viewed from side.

10. Do not remove feathering except that which hangs on floor between arrows numbered "10."

11. If very long curls are seen on or behind elbows when dog is viewed from front, remove with stripping comb only that hair which curls. Flatten remainder by brushing.

12. With stripping comb, take out enough hair to remove bushy look. Blend short hairs gradually from point numbered "1" into long hair below arrow numbered "12."

Remove whiskers. Trim off any long or unsightly hairs at corners of mouth and any particularly long hairs at inside corners of eyes. If cheek trimming needs blending, use thinning shears or stripping comb. Short hair on muzzle and front of legs needs no trimming. Thorough brushing will remove dead hair and make coat glisten with sheen and look of good health and well being.

Comb to keep coat free from tangles, using coarse toothed comb on feathering, finer comb on body coat. After first trim, bathe dog, and, to lay coat and make future grooming easier, pin large turkish towel around body (one pin under neck and another under loin).

For field work (not for breed ring) long hair on ears, brisket, legs, and under part of body may be removed closely to avoid its being torn or becoming snarled and tangled.

Tools

Combs—one with rather coarse teeth, one with finer teeth.
Clippers.
Thinning shears.
Scissors with blunted points.

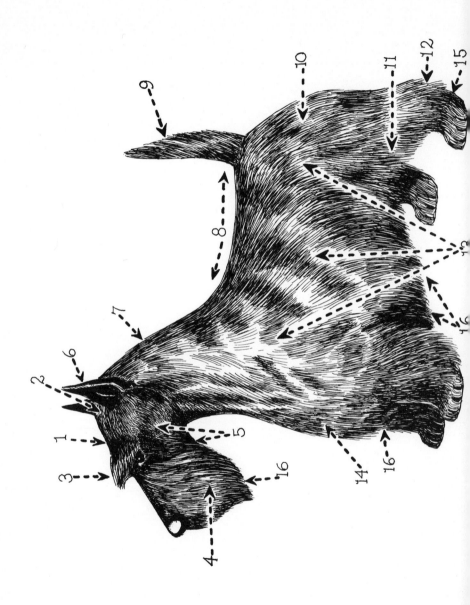

SCOTTISH TERRIER

1. Clip hair of skull, leaving hair one-eighth inch in length in area from stop to within one inch of occiput. Clean stop.
2. Trim hair on occiput to length of about one inch and blend into longer coat of neck.
3. Taper eyebrows gradually from one-quarter inch in length at outer corner to one inch in length at inner corner.
4. Trim whiskers to blend into sides of skull. Brush whiskers forward.
5. Clip cheeks and underjaw cleanly but blend at cheek into start of whiskers to avoid sharp dividing line.
6. Clip ears cleanly to point, leaving one inch of hair at base to make ears look smaller. With scissors, trim edges of ears neatly.
7. Trim neck hair neatly to about one inch in length, following contour of dog's neck. Blend hair at base of neck into coat of withers.
8. On back, from withers to tail, trim hair level.
9. Trim tail, tapering to point, leaving thick at base.
10. Trim hindquarters to roundness, emphasizing suggestion of power.
11. Trim hair of stifle in curve to show action and power of leg.
12. Leave furnishings on back but trim neatly, removing long hairs from insides of legs.
13. On shoulders, sides, and rump, trim hair so it is shorter on back, gradually becoming longer over ribs and sides. Blend to avoid sharp dividing line.
14. On chest, trim hair to breastbone, and remove overlong hair from below breastbone.
15. Remove excess hair from between toes and with scissors, trim edges of feet to neat roundness.
16. Do not remove furnishings, but thin excess hair. Trim only to neaten outline.

Tools

Stripping comb.
Steel comb.

Scissors with blunted points.
Clippers.

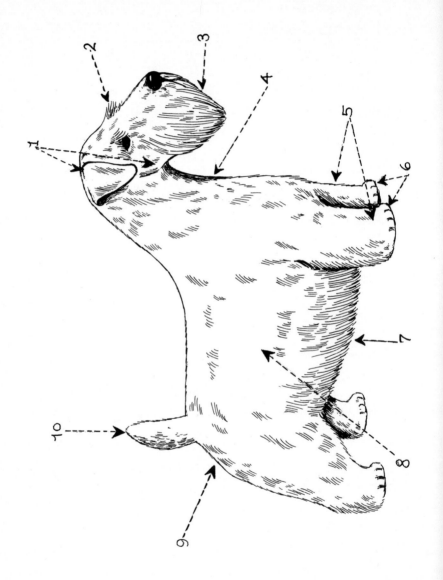

SEALYHAM TERRIER

1. Pluck or strip head, cheeks, and ears closely to achieve smooth silhouette.

2. Leave eyebrows bushy to shade eyes but not conceal them.

3. Even beard but not to shorten. Blend long hairs of whiskers into cleanly plucked or stripped cheeks.

4. Pluck or strip long hairs from throat, blending into coat of brisket.

5. Comb hair of forelegs to give appearance of little round posts. Do not trim.

6. With scissors, remove excess hair from between toes, and shape feet to neat roundness.

7. Leave hair of furnishings as long as possible to emphasize close-to-ground style of Sealyham.

8. Blend hair of sides from shorter hair of back to long hair of furnishings under body.

9. With scissors, trim hair closely in area immediately under tail, blending into longer hair of thighs.

10. Shape tail to pointed tip, with tail hair moderate length but without plume.

11. Blend hair of neck smoothly from head to withers and into back where hair is thick, coarse, and rather long. Trim back fine and level.

Tools

Metal comb.
Scissors with blunted points.
Stripping comb.

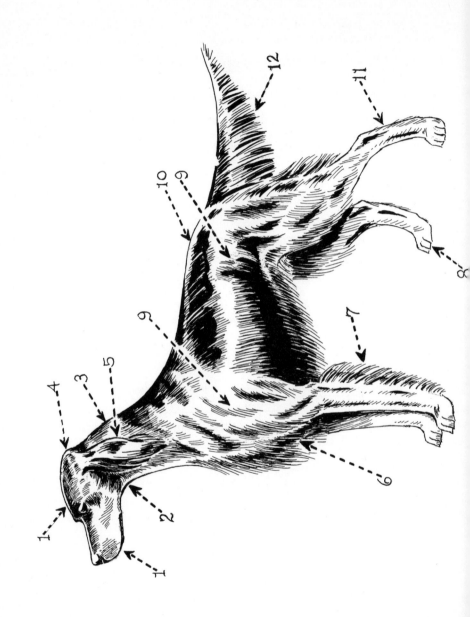

IRISH SETTER

1. With scissors, remove whiskers and long hair over eyes, producing clean-cut outline and seemingly adding length to head. Strip any rough ragged hairs from muzzle, cheeks, and skull.

2. Throat may be clipped very closely approximately two months prior to show so that coat will have grown back to be short and smooth by show-time. Or hair on throat may be trimmed and thinned closely and evenly, as throatiness is very undesirable. Taper hair of throat smoothly into body coat, leaving hair longer as trimming proceeds downward toward breastbone.

3. With stripping comb, smooth coat of nape or crest of neck to produce well-arched look.

4. Trim occiput to emphasize prominence. Accentuate slight dip just behind occiput where head joins neck.

5. Trim hair on top third of ear closely and smoothly. Strip excess hair from underside of ear and where ear joins head. If necessary, thin coat on lower two-thirds of ear where hair should be fine, straight, and having a guard coat extending at least an inch below leather.

6. Do not remove under-furnishings. Hair should be long and straight, emphasizing great depth of chest, but without business.

7. Comb down feathering on back of forelegs and trim only to even outline.

8. Trim hair around feet to neaten outline and make feet seem to point straight forward. Avoid cutting unevenly.

9. Thin lightly to remove any bulges on shoulders, smoothing any rough coat. Trim loin sparingly to show slight tuck-up, but do not emphasize.

10. On Setters that appear "overbuilt" (high at hips) with low tail placement, thin coat slightly over hips. To prevent gouging, insert thinning shears diagonally, well under coat, coming in from ends of hair. Cut some of undercoat, then comb it out. In Irish Setters with a "two-shade" coat that is lighter underneath, excessive stripping will produce an uneven, displeasing combination of light and dark hairs.

11. Leave scant feathering on hocks but trim to even outline.

12. Taper the long straight tail feathering gracefully from pointed tip of tail toward dog's body. To reduce bushiness, thin lightly with stripping comb.

Tools

Comb.
Brush.
Stripping comb.
Clippers.
Thinning shears.
Scissors with blunted points.

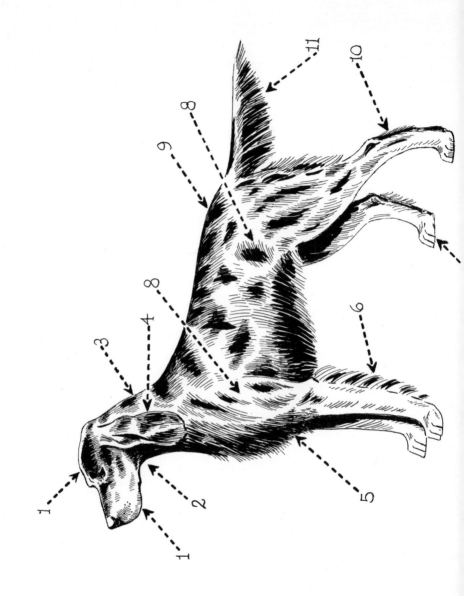

GORDON SETTER

1. With scissors, remove whiskers and long hair over eyes, producing clean-cut outline and seemingly adding length to head. Strip any rough ragged hairs from muzzle, cheeks, and skull.

2. Throat may be clipped very closely approximately two months prior to show so that coat will have grown back to be short and smooth by show-time, or hair on throat may be trimmed and thinned closely and evenly, as throatiness is very undesirable. Taper hair of throat smoothly into body coat, leaving hair longer as trimming proceeds downward toward breastbone.

3. With stripping comb, smooth coat of nape, or crest, of neck to produce well-arched look.

4. Trim hair on top third of ear closely and smoothly. Strip excess hair from underside of ear and where ear joins head. If necessary, thin coat on lower two-thirds of ear where hair should be fine, straight, and having a guard coat extending at least an inch below leather.

5. Do not remove under-furnishings. Hair should be long and straight, emphasizing great depth of chest, but without bushiness.

6. Comb down feathering on back of forelegs and trim only to even outline.

7. Trim hair around feet to neaten outline and make feet seem to point straight forward. Avoid cutting unevenly.

8. Thin lightly to remove any bulges on shoulders, smoothing any rough coat. Trim loin sparingly to show slight tuck-up, but do not emphasize.

9. On Setters that appear "overbuilt" (high at hips) with low tail placement, thin coat slightly over hips. To prevent gouging, insert thinning shears diagonally, well under coat, coming in from ends of hair. Cut some of undercoat, then comb it out.

10. Leave scant feathering on hocks but trim to even outline.

11. Taper the long straight tail feathering gracefully from pointed tip of tail toward dog's body. To reduce bushiness, thin lightly with stripping comb.

Tools

Comb.
Brush.
Stripping comb.
Clippers.
Thinning shears.
Scissors with blunted points.

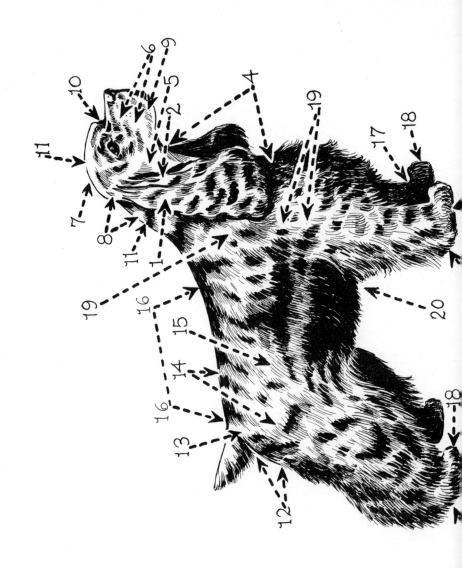

COCKER SPANIEL

1. Clip from arrow numbered "1" upward and around line of skull to approximate center of head. If skull appears broad, clip closely at sides. If skull appears narrow, build up by allowing hair to fill in on sides of skull.

2. Clip underside of ears cleanly. From arrow numbered "1" strip upward and forward.

3. Repeat same operations on opposite side of head.

4. Starting at breastbone, clip upward on neck and throat to underside of lower jaw and continue forward to end of jaw.

5. Continue working upward and forward, clipping hair on cheeks and forward along muzzle to nose, following outline of bone structure.

6. Working back from nose, trim out to eye sockets.

7. From occiput, clip forward cleanly down the stop. Avoid excessive build-up of hair over eyebrows and forward part of skull, resulting in false appearance of well-rounded dome.

8. Starting at base of skull, clip along sides of neck, being sure to blend smoothly into shoulders and form clean pattern over withers.

9. Using scissors, remove feelers on both sides of muzzle. Clean up rough spots on lip and underside of lower jaw. Blend hair of withers into hair of neck.

10. Using scissors, remove long eyebrows and trim eyelashes close to eyelids.

11. Using short strokes with straight safety razor with lay of coat, smooth out all rough spots on top of skull and neck.

12. Using clippers, clean out hair under tail between arrows numbered "12," clipping from lower point upward.

13. With thinning shears, blend hair of tail into rump.

14. Using thinning shears, clean off hips and rump to give well-rounded appearance.

15. Use thinning shears to clean out flanks so they are trim and free of wild hairs.

16. To present the best possible appearance, thin out top line with thinning shears from withers to set-on of tail. Avoid indiscriminate use of thinning shears, which may accentuate soft back, too high rump, or poor set-on of tail.

17. Clean out excess hair to show strong pasterns.

18. With dog standing firmly on all four feet, trim feet to neat, well-rounded shape. Clean out excess hair at back of feet and trim off flush with pads, but avoid trimming so closely as to give appearance of cat feet. Trim hair between pads.

19. Using razor, strip shoulders with short strokes, blending into forelegs and spring of ribs.

20. Using scissors and starting at forelegs, trim under-feathering to provide light under the dog. Taper feathering upward to flank.

Tools

Clippers (hand or electric).
Wire brush.
Comb.
Straight-handled safety razor.
Thinning shears (notched on one blade only).
Scissors with blunted points.

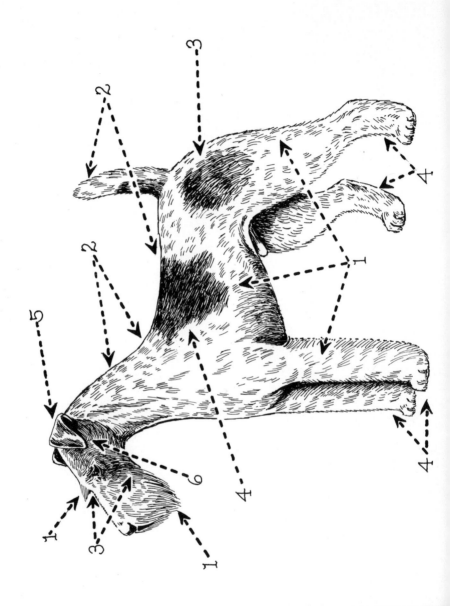

WIRE-HAIRED FOX TERRIER

1. Do not remove completely, but reduce length and density of leg hair, eyebrows, face hair, and whiskers by pulling out longest and oldest hair. Take down rib hair closer than leg hair. Brush coat well every day to stimulate growth and encourage hair to lay properly.

2. Stripping should be started on neck, withers, tail, and back about three weeks after stripping areas described in "1," above, and should also be brushed well to encourage coat in these parts to lay in with areas previously stripped. In stripping tail, take care neither to remove too much hair nor to remove too little.

3. Strip areas numbered "3" about a week or ten days after stripping areas numbered "2." Blend hair where areas previously stripped join one another and where they join portions of coat numbered "3." Also, remove any long or straggly hairs that now appear to spoil outline in parts of coat previously stripped.

4. Blend along edges and strip areas numbered "4" about two weeks after areas numbered "3." Again go over parts of coat previously stripped, removing any undesirable growth, but take care not to remove too much hair and to shape coat to follow body conformation. Shape feet by plucking, stripping, and trimming down to sole level. With scissors, round out edges and level off long hair under feet. At this time the dog should be bathed.

5. The ears should be taken down cleanly a few days after completing areas numbered "4." Pull out hair from ears. *Do not cut* ear hair, for color and carriage of ears are affected by using such incorrect procedure at this stage. Pull out hair inside ears. Using tweezers, carefully remove hair down in ear canal. In many instances ears are poorly carried simply because the hair in the ear canal is not removed. And, even worse, hair

that is not removed from ear canal will hold matter that causes infection and possibly canker.

It is most important to go over the entire coat at this time, stripping and grooming to correct previous grooming in relation to the dog as a whole. Shape the stifle and elbow areas slightly, making sure that there is no suggestion of exaggeration in these parts. Hair at elbows should never be taken out in normal maintenance grooming as shoulders may appear exaggerated, giving impression that dog is out at elbows. In shaping stifle, a slight suggestion of bowed legs is desirable, but suggestion must be only *slight*. Remove hair at bend of stifle, first having dog standing sidewise to trimmer, then with dog standing with back toward trimmer so that view is same as that presented in breed ring to judge as dog moves away from him.

6. Trim cheeks and skull, blending from high point of cheeks forward in a line to the nose. Look at dog full-face and take care not to remove too much hair from under eye. Removing too much hair under eye is common fault in trimming that causes dog to look snipey, or, in some cases, bold in eye.

To keep the dog in good coat for the longest possible time, go over the dog every three or four days and adjust the shape according to the rate of growth. Coat texture may be controlled by raking out *a little* of the undercoat, as necessary.

Tools

Steel comb without handle, preferably with teeth not too thin and about one-eighth inch apart.
Chalk.
Stripping comb.
Bristle brush.
Rubber grooming pad with steel pins.
Hound glove with hair—*not* wire—bristles.
Scissors with blunted points.

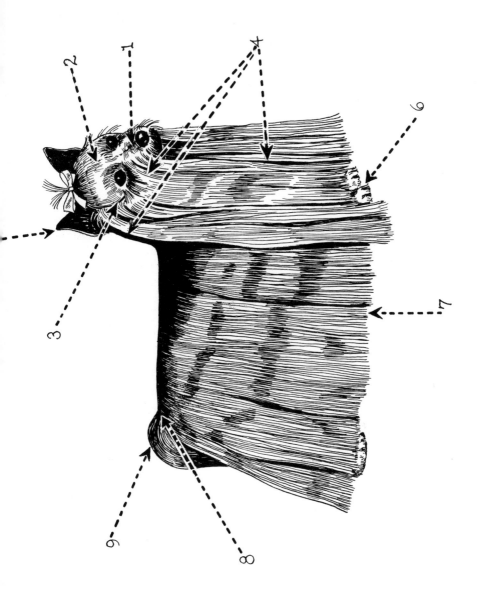

YORKSHIRE TERRIER

1. Part hair from end of nose to tip of tail. Brush to either side, removing all tangles.

2. With hair on head parted in center, tie fall with tiny ribbon on either side. Or tie with one ribbon as illustrated, "fall" to hang either back of head or forward.

3. Divide hair at eye-set and part from corner of eye to top inside of ear, then straight across.

4. Brush "fall" downward. It is important to have good length of moustache on muzzle and head.

5. On outside of ear, trim hair down about one inch. Also, remove all hair from inside of ear and from edges if necessary.

6. Trim fringe on feet to follow outline of feet and give neat rounded appearance. Cut out hair between pads.

7. Brush body coat straight down on each side so that it hangs close to body and straight as a string.

8. Part hair diagonally from tail-set to rear, keeping square look to body.

9. Brush tail feathering down close to rear.

The grooming of the Yorkshire Terrier is of the utmost importance for in the breed ring more points are allotted to the coat than to the coat of any other breed. Starting in puppyhood, the Yorkshire Terrier should be taught to lie on his back in his owner's lap for daily brushing under the chin, legs, and stomach.

To encourage growth and improve condition, hair may be wrapped in strips of silk or in wax paper. After sectioning off coat, apply small amount of oil and fold each individual section of hair in a piece of waxed paper or strip of silk, then secure with a rubber band wound around twice. To develop a show coat, hair should be wrapped after each daily grooming, not to wave the hair but rather to protect it and to keep it from breaking, matting, or becoming soiled.

Tools

Brush having long or medium length bristles (special Yorkshire Terrier brushes available in England).
Comb having blunt teeth.
Scissors with blunted points.

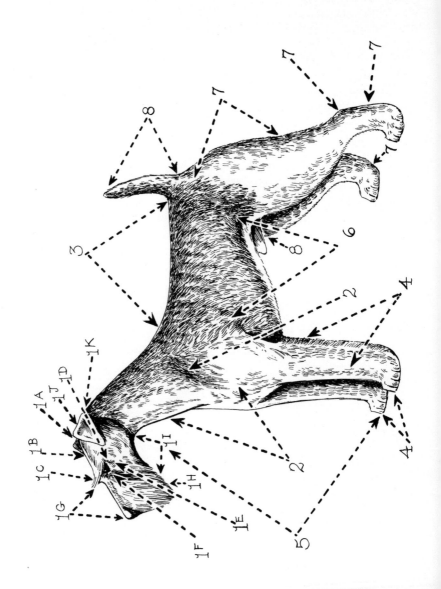

WELSH TERRIER

1-A. Trim head to show flatness and strength between ears, as distinguished from head of Wire-Haired Fox Terrier.

1-B. Trim skull very closely.

1-C. Trim eyebrows so that they are moderately heavy over inside corner of each eye, gradually tapering to lesser amount of hair at outside corner, but leaving sufficient hair to give Terrier a hard-bitten look.

1-D. Trim eyebrows neatly and closely over outside corner of each eye so there is no break in the line.

1-E. Trim cheeks closely from outside corners of eyes to corners of mouth so as to show powerful, clean-cut depth of jaw.

1-F. Trim hair in front of eye to corner of mouth short and evenly.

1-G. To give straight line from top of skull to point of nose, trim hair on top of muzzle from slight stop between eyebrows to nose.

1-H. Leave chin whiskers moderately profuse, but not exaggerated.

1-I. Clean underjaw from corners of mouth back to neck line.

1-J. Clip ears closely on outside and remove all hair on inside.

1-K. With scissors straighten hair on edges of ears to give clean V-shape.

2. From closely clipped neck line in front, trim and even hair down over brisket, leaving coat about one-half inch longer as you trim to brisket, where front legs join body. Trim sides and front of shoulders closely and neatly.

3. From withers, over back, to tail-set, trim hair evenly but not so closely as on neck.

127

4. Trim hair on front legs to absolute straightness, with most of hair evened and removed from back line of legs. Even hair of legs in front and on sides where it joins hair of body and shoulders, blending to form unbroken line. Shape hair of feet to roundness. Remove all superfluous hair between toes and on edges of pads.

5. Check correctness of trimming of front, which should be series of straight lines: from top of shoulders to feet; from brisket to tips of toes; and from chin line to middle of neck. Adjust length of hair as necessary.

6. Shape chest cage from closely trimmed back to slightly longer hair on sides; taper gradually into heavy but evenly trimmed coat on under portion of chest. On chest floor, remove only discolored hair or uneven hair, preventing appearance of shagginess. Trim sides of chest to follow body line. With scissors, taper hair from chest to loin closely, emphasizing tuck-up. On belly, remove only shaggy or matted hairs—do not shave this part.

7. From closely trimmed back line, trim hair to taper gradually to blend into moderately heavily coated first and second thighs. Trim only unsightly or shaggy hair from first thigh to hock joint. Trim back line of hock straight and remove any shaggy or discolored hairs from between rear legs, giving clean, unbroken lines from pelvic junction to feet.

8. Trim tail evenly and neatly to a tip toward the head. Trim fine undercoat where tail joins stern. Clean off long unsightly hairs around genitals.

Tools

Clippers.
Wide-toothed comb.
Scissors with blunted points.